REVITALIZING YOUR LIVER

A Comprehensive Diet and lifestyle Guide for Managing Liver Health

ETHAN WALKER

All Rights Reserved. No part of this publication may be reproduced, distributed, or transmitted in any form or by any means, including photocopying, recording or other electronic or mechanical methods, without the prior written permission of the publisher, except in the case of brief quotations, embodied in critical reviews and certain other non-commercial uses permitted by copyright law.

Contents

Welcome to the Revitalizing your Liver 4
   How to Use This Cookbook 4
   A Note on Nutritional Information 5
Chapter 1: Understanding Liver Health 7
   Anatomy and Function of the Liver 7
   Key Roles in Metabolism and Detoxification 8
Chapter 2: Common Liver Diseases 11
   Fatty Liver Disease (NAFLD and AFLD) 11
   Hepatitis (A, B, C) 15
   Cirrhosis 21
   Liver Cancer 27
Chapter 3: Causes of Liver Diseases 33
   Lifestyle Factors 33
   Environmental Factors 37
   Genetic Factors 42
   Other Health Conditions 46
Chapter 4: Prevention and Solutions for Common Liver Diseases 52
   Dietary Changes 52
   Lifestyle Modifications 54
   Medical Treatments 55
Chapter 5: Liver-Friendly Breakfast Recipes 59
   Smoothie Bowls 59
   Oatmeal Variations 61
   Liver-Friendly Pancakes 62
   Egg-Based Dishes 65

   Whole Grain Toasts..66

Chapter 6: Liver-Friendly Lunch Recipes..69

   Salads and Bowls...69

   Soups and Stews...74

   Wraps and Sandwiches..80

Chapter 7: Liver-Friendly Dinner Recipes...86

   Main Courses...86

   Side dishes...94

   Healthy Desserts...99

Chapter 8: Liver-Friendly Drinks and Beverages Recipes.........................104

Chapter 9: 30 Day Liver-Friendly Meal Plan..111

   Introduction to The 30-Day Meal Plan for a Liver-Friendly Diet............111

   Week 1: Detox and Reset..116

   Week 2: Nutrient Boost...120

   Week 3: Balance and Sustain...124

Chapter 10: Lifestyle Methods for a Healthy Liver....................................135

   Exercise and Physical Activity..135

   Stress Management..141

   Avoiding Toxins...147

   Regular Medical Check-Ups...152

Chapter 11: Conclusion: Embracing a Healthy Liver Lifestyle..................158

Welcome to the Revitalizing your Liver

Welcome to "Revitalizing your Liver" your comprehensive guide to nurturing and maintaining one of the most vital organs in your body – the liver. This cookbook is designed not only to provide you with delicious and nutritious recipes but also to educate you on the importance of liver health, the common diseases that can affect the liver, and practical lifestyle changes to support this essential organ. Whether you're looking to improve your liver function, manage a liver condition, or simply lead a healthier life, this book is your go-to resource.

How to Use This Cookbook

"The Healthy Liver Diet" is structured to guide you seamlessly through understanding liver health, preventing liver diseases, and adopting a liver-friendly lifestyle. Here's how to make the most out of this cookbook:

1. **Educational Foundation**: Start by reading the first section on understanding liver health and common liver diseases. This will give you a solid foundation of why liver health is crucial and what factors contribute to liver-related conditions.

2. **30-Day Meal Plan**: Move on to the 30-day meal plan, which is divided into four weeks, each with a specific focus such as detoxification, nutrient boosting, balance, and maintenance. This plan is designed to help you reset and rejuvenate your liver with carefully curated meals.

3. **Recipes**: Dive into the extensive collection of liver-friendly recipes. These are categorized into breakfast, lunch, and dinner, making it easy to plan your meals. Each recipe is crafted to be both delicious and beneficial for liver health, utilizing ingredients known for their liver-supportive properties.

4. **Lifestyle Tips**: Incorporate the lifestyle methods outlined in the final section of the book. These include exercise recommendations, stress management techniques, and tips for avoiding environmental toxins, all of which contribute to a healthier liver.

5. **Ongoing Reference**: Use the glossary and resource sections to further your knowledge and keep up with the latest research and recommendations on liver health.

By following this structure, you will not only learn about liver health but also how to implement practical and sustainable changes in your diet and lifestyle to support your liver and overall health.

A Note on Nutritional Information

Nutrition plays a critical role in liver health, and this cookbook emphasizes nutrient-dense foods that support liver function. Each recipe includes nutritional information to help you make informed choices about what you're eating. Here's what to look for:

- **Calories**: Understanding caloric intake helps manage weight, which is crucial for liver health, especially in preventing and managing fatty liver disease.

- **Macronutrients**: The balance of carbohydrates, proteins, and fats is essential for metabolic health. This cookbook focuses on healthy fats, lean proteins, and complex carbohydrates.

- **Micronutrients**: Vitamins and minerals are vital for liver function. Recipes are rich in liver-supportive nutrients such as vitamins A, C, D, E, and B-complex, as well as minerals like zinc, magnesium, and selenium.

- **Fiber**: High-fiber foods aid in digestion and help the liver by promoting regular bowel movements, which is a natural way to eliminate toxins.

- **Antioxidants**: Many recipes include ingredients high in antioxidants, which protect the liver from oxidative stress and inflammation.

By paying attention to these nutritional aspects, you can ensure that your diet not only supports liver health but also enhances your overall wellness.

Welcome to a journey of better liver health through delicious food and a mindful lifestyle. Let's get started on the path to a healthier, happier you!

Chapter 1: Understanding Liver Health

Anatomy and Function of the Liver

Overview of Liver Functions

The liver, the largest internal organ in the human body, weighs about three pounds and is located in the upper right quadrant of the abdomen, just below the diaphragm. Its remarkable structure comprises two main lobes, each further divided into lobules, which are connected by a network of bile ducts. This intricate organ performs over 500 vital functions, making it indispensable to overall health and well-being.

At its core, the liver acts as a multifunctional powerhouse, playing essential roles in digestion, metabolism, detoxification, and immune defense. Here's an overview of its primary functions:

1. **Bile Production and Excretion**: The liver produces bile, a yellow-green fluid essential for digesting fats. Bile is stored in the gallbladder and released into the small intestine to emulsify fats, facilitating their absorption.

2. **Metabolism of Carbohydrates, Proteins, and Fats**: The liver regulates blood sugar levels by storing glucose as glycogen and converting it back into glucose when needed. It also processes amino acids from protein digestion and converts excess carbohydrates and proteins into fats for storage.

3. **Detoxification and Filtration**: One of the liver's most critical functions is detoxifying the blood. It filters out toxins, drugs, and other harmful substances, converting them into less harmful compounds that can be excreted by the kidneys or intestines.

4. **Synthesis of Plasma Proteins**: The liver produces important proteins such as albumin, which maintains blood volume and pressure, and clotting factors necessary for blood coagulation.

5. **Storage of Vitamins and Minerals**: The liver stores essential vitamins like A, D, E, K, and B12, as well as minerals such as iron and copper, releasing them into the bloodstream as needed.

6. **Immune Function**: The liver contains Kupffer cells, a type of macrophage that helps remove pathogens and debris from the blood, playing a crucial role in immune defense.

7. **Hormone Regulation**: The liver metabolizes and regulates hormones, including sex hormones and thyroid hormones, ensuring their proper levels in the bloodstream.

Key Roles in Metabolism and Detoxification

The liver's involvement in metabolism and detoxification is perhaps its most renowned function, with profound impacts on overall health. Let's delve deeper into these roles:

Metabolism

1. **Carbohydrate Metabolism**:
    - **Glycogenesis**: When blood glucose levels are high, the liver converts excess glucose into glycogen for storage.
    - **Glycogenolysis**: During fasting or between meals, the liver breaks down glycogen into glucose, releasing it into the bloodstream to maintain energy levels.
    - **Gluconeogenesis**: The liver can produce glucose from non-carbohydrate sources such as amino acids and glycerol,

ensuring a continuous energy supply, especially during prolonged fasting or intense exercise.

2. **Protein Metabolism**:
   - **Amino Acid Processing**: The liver deaminates amino acids, removing the amino group to use them for energy or convert them into other necessary molecules.
   - **Urea Cycle**: The liver converts the toxic ammonia produced during amino acid breakdown into urea, which is then excreted by the kidneys.

3. **Lipid Metabolism**:
   - **Fatty Acid Oxidation**: The liver breaks down fatty acids to produce energy.
   - **Lipoprotein Synthesis**: It produces lipoproteins, which transport lipids in the bloodstream.
   - **Cholesterol Synthesis and Regulation**: The liver synthesizes cholesterol, a vital component of cell membranes and precursor for steroid hormones, and regulates its levels in the blood.

Detoxification

1. **Biotransformation**:
   - **Phase I Reactions**: The liver uses enzymes, primarily from the cytochrome P450 family, to oxidize, reduce, or hydrolyze toxins, drugs, and other harmful substances, making them more water-soluble.
   - **Phase II Reactions**: These modified substances are then conjugated with other compounds like glucuronic acid, sulfuric acid, or glutathione, further increasing their solubility and preparing them for excretion.

2. **Ammonia Detoxification:**
   - Ammonia, a byproduct of protein metabolism, is highly toxic. The liver converts ammonia into urea through the urea cycle, which is then safely excreted by the kidneys.

3. **Alcohol Metabolism:**
   - The liver metabolizes alcohol through enzymes such as alcohol dehydrogenase and aldehyde dehydrogenase, converting it into less toxic substances like acetaldehyde and acetate, which are eventually broken down into carbon dioxide and water.

4. **Drug Metabolism:**
   - The liver processes pharmaceuticals, breaking them down into metabolites that can be easily eliminated. This function is crucial for drug efficacy and safety, as it ensures drugs do not accumulate to toxic levels in the body.

5. **Hormone Degradation:**
   - The liver breaks down and removes excess hormones from the bloodstream, maintaining hormonal balance and preventing potential disruptions in body functions.

The liver's roles in metabolism and detoxification highlight its significance in maintaining homeostasis and overall health. By efficiently processing nutrients, detoxifying harmful substances, and regulating biochemical pathways, the liver ensures that the body functions smoothly and remains resilient against various internal and external challenges.

Understanding the anatomy and functions of the liver underscores the importance of adopting lifestyle and dietary practices that support liver health. Through this cookbook, you'll discover how to nourish this vital organ with liver-friendly foods and habits, paving the way for a healthier, more vibrant life.

Chapter 2: Common Liver Diseases

Fatty Liver Disease (NAFLD and AFLD)

Fatty liver disease, a condition characterized by the accumulation of fat in liver cells, is increasingly common worldwide. It comes in two primary forms: Non-Alcoholic Fatty Liver Disease (NAFLD) and Alcoholic Fatty Liver Disease (AFLD). Understanding the causes, symptoms, diagnosis, and treatment options for these conditions is crucial for managing and preventing their progression.

Non-Alcoholic Fatty Liver Disease (NAFLD)

Causes: NAFLD is primarily associated with metabolic syndrome and lifestyle factors rather than alcohol consumption. Key causes include:

- **Obesity**: Excess body weight, particularly abdominal fat, significantly increases the risk of NAFLD.
- **Insulin Resistance**: Often linked with type 2 diabetes and obesity, insulin resistance causes fat accumulation in the liver.
- **Dyslipidemia**: Elevated levels of triglycerides and low-density lipoprotein (LDL) cholesterol contribute to liver fat deposition.
- **Poor Diet**: Diets high in refined carbohydrates, saturated fats, and sugary beverages promote fat accumulation in the liver.
- **Sedentary Lifestyle**: Lack of physical activity exacerbates weight gain and metabolic syndrome, leading to NAFLD.
- **Genetics**: Genetic predisposition can make some individuals more susceptible to developing NAFLD.

Symptoms: NAFLD is often asymptomatic, particularly in its early stages. However, as the disease progresses, symptoms may include:

- **Fatigue**: Persistent tiredness and lack of energy.
- **Abdominal Discomfort**: Mild pain or discomfort in the upper right abdomen.
- **Enlarged Liver**: Hepatomegaly, or an enlarged liver, detected through physical examination.
- **Unexplained Weight Loss**: In more advanced stages, unintended weight loss may occur.

Diagnosis: Diagnosing NAFLD involves a combination of medical history, physical examination, and diagnostic tests:

- **Medical History**: Evaluation of risk factors such as obesity, diabetes, and dietary habits.
- **Physical Examination**: Palpation to check for liver enlargement and other physical signs.
- **Blood Tests**: Liver function tests (LFTs) to measure enzymes like ALT and AST, which may be elevated in NAFLD.
- **Imaging Studies**: Ultrasound, CT scan, or MRI to visualize fat accumulation in the liver.
- **Liver Biopsy**: In some cases, a liver biopsy may be performed to assess the extent of liver damage and rule out other conditions.

Treatment Options: There is no specific medication for NAFLD, but lifestyle modifications are the cornerstone of treatment:

- **Weight Loss**: Gradual weight loss through a combination of diet and exercise can significantly reduce liver fat.

- **Healthy Diet**: A balanced diet rich in fruits, vegetables, whole grains, lean proteins, and healthy fats. Reducing intake of sugary and high-fat foods is essential.

- **Regular Exercise**: Engaging in at least 150 minutes of moderate-intensity exercise per week helps improve liver health.

- **Managing Comorbidities**: Controlling diabetes, hypertension, and dyslipidemia through medication and lifestyle changes.

- **Avoiding Alcohol**: Abstaining from alcohol to prevent further liver damage.

- **Medications**: In some cases, doctors may prescribe medications to manage underlying conditions like diabetes and dyslipidemia that contribute to NAFLD.

Alcoholic Fatty Liver Disease (AFLD)

Causes: AFLD is directly caused by excessive alcohol consumption. Factors influencing its development include:

- **Quantity of Alcohol**: The risk increases with the amount and frequency of alcohol intake.

- **Duration of Drinking**: Prolonged alcohol use over several years leads to cumulative liver damage.

- **Genetics**: Genetic factors can influence an individual's susceptibility to alcohol-induced liver damage.

- **Gender**: Women are more susceptible to AFLD at lower levels of alcohol consumption compared to men.

- **Nutritional Deficiencies**: Poor nutrition, often seen in heavy drinkers, exacerbates liver damage.

Symptoms: Like NAFLD, AFLD can be asymptomatic in its early stages. As the disease progresses, symptoms may include:

- **Fatigue**: Persistent tiredness and lethargy.
- **Abdominal Pain**: Discomfort or pain in the upper right quadrant of the abdomen.
- **Jaundice**: Yellowing of the skin and eyes, indicating more advanced liver damage.
- **Swollen Abdomen**: Ascites, or fluid accumulation in the abdomen, in severe cases.
- **Nausea and Vomiting**: Digestive disturbances may occur.

Diagnosis: Diagnosing AFLD involves similar methods as NAFLD but with a focus on alcohol consumption history:

- **Medical History**: Detailed inquiry into the patient's alcohol consumption patterns.
- **Physical Examination**: Checking for signs of liver disease such as jaundice and liver enlargement.
- **Blood Tests**: Liver function tests (LFTs) to assess liver enzyme levels.
- **Imaging Studies**: Ultrasound, CT scan, or MRI to detect liver fat and assess liver structure.
- **Liver Biopsy**: In certain cases, a biopsy may be necessary to confirm the diagnosis and evaluate the extent of liver damage.

Treatment Options: The primary treatment for AFLD is abstinence from alcohol. Additional treatment measures include:

- **Alcohol Abstinence**: Complete cessation of alcohol intake is crucial to halt and potentially reverse liver damage.

- **Nutritional Support**: Ensuring adequate nutrition to support liver regeneration and overall health.

- **Medications**: In some cases, medications may be prescribed to manage withdrawal symptoms and prevent relapse.

- **Liver Transplant**: In severe cases of AFLD leading to liver failure, a liver transplant may be necessary.

- **Support Groups**: Participation in support groups like Alcoholics Anonymous (AA) can provide ongoing support for maintaining sobriety.

Both NAFLD and AFLD highlight the liver's vulnerability to lifestyle factors and underscore the importance of early detection, lifestyle modification, and ongoing medical management. By understanding these common liver diseases, individuals can take proactive steps to protect their liver health and prevent the progression of these conditions.

Hepatitis (A, B, C)

Hepatitis refers to inflammation of the liver and is often caused by viral infections. The three most common types are Hepatitis A, B, and C. Each type is caused by a different virus, has unique modes of transmission, presents with varying symptoms, and requires distinct approaches to diagnosis and treatment.

Hepatitis A

Causes: Hepatitis A is caused by the Hepatitis A virus (HAV), which is primarily transmitted through ingestion of contaminated food or water. It can also spread through close personal contact with an infected person. The virus is prevalent in areas with poor sanitation and hygiene practices.

Symptoms: The symptoms of Hepatitis A usually appear a few weeks after exposure to the virus and can range from mild to severe. Common symptoms include:

- **Fatigue**: Persistent tiredness and weakness.
- **Nausea and Vomiting**: Digestive disturbances.
- **Abdominal Pain**: Discomfort in the upper right abdomen.
- **Loss of Appetite**: Reduced desire to eat.
- **Jaundice**: Yellowing of the skin and eyes.
- **Dark Urine**: Brownish urine indicating liver dysfunction.
- **Clay-Colored Stools**: Pale stools due to lack of bile.
- **Fever**: Mild to moderate fever.

Diagnosis: Diagnosis of Hepatitis A involves a combination of medical history, physical examination, and specific tests:

- **Medical History**: Evaluation of potential exposure to contaminated food, water, or close contact with an infected person.
- **Physical Examination**: Checking for signs of jaundice and abdominal tenderness.
- **Blood Tests**: Detection of anti-HAV IgM antibodies, which indicate recent infection with the Hepatitis A virus.

Treatment Options: There is no specific treatment for Hepatitis A, as it is a self-limiting disease that usually resolves on its own. Management focuses on supportive care:

- **Rest**: Adequate rest to support the body's immune response.
- **Hydration**: Maintaining fluid intake to prevent dehydration.
- **Nutrition**: Consuming a balanced diet to support recovery.
- **Avoiding Alcohol and Drugs**: Refraining from substances that can further stress the liver.
- **Vaccination**: The Hepatitis A vaccine is highly effective in preventing infection and is recommended for people traveling to areas with high HAV prevalence or at higher risk of exposure.

Hepatitis B

Causes: Hepatitis B is caused by the Hepatitis B virus (HBV), which is transmitted through contact with infectious body fluids such as blood, semen, and vaginal secretions. Common modes of transmission include:

- **Unprotected Sexual Contact**: Engaging in unprotected sex with an infected person.
- **Sharing Needles**: Using contaminated needles or syringes, often associated with intravenous drug use.
- **Mother-to-Child Transmission**: Passing the virus from an infected mother to her baby during childbirth.
- **Occupational Exposure**: Healthcare workers and others exposed to blood and body fluids are at higher risk.

Symptoms: Symptoms of Hepatitis B can range from mild to severe and may not appear until several months after infection. They include:

- **Fatigue**: Persistent tiredness and weakness.
- **Fever**: Mild to moderate fever.
- **Joint Pain**: Aching joints.
- **Abdominal Pain**: Discomfort in the upper right abdomen.
- **Loss of Appetite**: Reduced desire to eat.
- **Nausea and Vomiting**: Digestive disturbances.
- **Jaundice**: Yellowing of the skin and eyes.
- **Dark Urine**: Brownish urine indicating liver dysfunction.
- **Clay-Colored Stools**: Pale stools due to lack of bile.

Diagnosis: Diagnosing Hepatitis B involves a combination of medical history, physical examination, and specific tests:

- **Medical History**: Evaluation of potential exposure to HBV through sexual contact, needle use, or occupational hazards.
- **Physical Examination**: Checking for signs of jaundice and abdominal tenderness.
- **Blood Tests**: Detection of HBsAg (Hepatitis B surface antigen), anti-HBc (Hepatitis B core antibody), and anti-HBs (Hepatitis B surface antibody).

Treatment Options: The treatment of Hepatitis B depends on whether the infection is acute or chronic:

- **Acute Hepatitis B**: Most adults with acute Hepatitis B recover without treatment, focusing on supportive care such as rest, hydration, and nutrition.

- **Chronic Hepatitis B**: Long-term treatment aims to reduce liver damage and prevent complications. Options include:
  - **Antiviral Medications**: Drugs such as tenofovir and entecavir help reduce the viral load and slow disease progression.
  - **Regular Monitoring**: Regular blood tests and liver ultrasounds to monitor liver function and detect early signs of liver damage.
  - **Liver Transplant**: In severe cases of liver failure, a liver transplant may be necessary.
  - **Vaccination**: The Hepatitis B vaccine is effective in preventing infection and is recommended for all infants, unvaccinated adults at risk, and healthcare workers.

Hepatitis C

Causes: Hepatitis C is caused by the Hepatitis C virus (HCV), primarily transmitted through contact with infected blood. Common modes of transmission include:

- **Sharing Needles**: Using contaminated needles or syringes, often associated with intravenous drug use.
- **Blood Transfusions**: Receiving blood transfusions or organ transplants before 1992, when widespread screening of the blood supply began.
- **Mother-to-Child Transmission**: Passing the virus from an infected mother to her baby during childbirth.
- **Occupational Exposure**: Healthcare workers and others exposed to blood and body fluids are at higher risk.

Symptoms: Hepatitis C is often asymptomatic in its early stages. When symptoms do occur, they may include:

- **Fatigue:** Persistent tiredness and weakness.
- **Fever:** Mild to moderate fever.
- **Joint Pain:** Aching joints.
- **Abdominal Pain:** Discomfort in the upper right abdomen.
- **Loss of Appetite:** Reduced desire to eat.
- **Nausea and Vomiting:** Digestive disturbances.
- **Jaundice:** Yellowing of the skin and eyes.
- **Dark Urine:** Brownish urine indicating liver dysfunction.
- **Clay-Colored Stools:** Pale stools due to lack of bile.

Diagnosis: Diagnosing Hepatitis C involves a combination of medical history, physical examination, and specific tests:

- **Medical History:** Evaluation of potential exposure to HCV through needle use, blood transfusions, or occupational hazards.
- **Physical Examination:** Checking for signs of jaundice and abdominal tenderness.
- **Blood Tests:** Detection of anti-HCV antibodies and HCV RNA to confirm the presence of the virus.

Treatment Options: The treatment of Hepatitis C has improved significantly with the development of direct-acting antiviral (DAA) medications:

- **Antiviral Medications**: DAAs such as sofosbuvir, ledipasvir, and daclatasvir have revolutionized Hepatitis C treatment, achieving high cure rates with shorter treatment durations and fewer side effects.

- **Regular Monitoring**: Regular blood tests to monitor liver function and viral load.

- **Liver Transplant**: In severe cases of liver failure, a liver transplant may be necessary.

- **Lifestyle Modifications**: Avoiding alcohol, eating a balanced diet, and maintaining a healthy weight to support liver health.

Hepatitis A, B, and C highlight the diverse etiologies and clinical presentations of viral hepatitis. Understanding their causes, symptoms, diagnosis, and treatment options is crucial for effective management and prevention. Through early detection, appropriate medical care, and lifestyle modifications, individuals can significantly reduce the impact of these conditions on their liver health and overall well-being.

Cirrhosis

Cirrhosis is a late-stage liver disease characterized by irreversible scarring (fibrosis) of the liver. This condition is the result of long-term, continuous damage to the liver and can lead to significant liver dysfunction. Understanding the causes, symptoms, diagnosis, and treatment options for cirrhosis is essential for managing and potentially slowing the progression of this debilitating disease.

Causes

Cirrhosis can develop from various chronic liver diseases and conditions that cause long-term liver damage. The most common causes include:

1. **Chronic Alcohol Abuse**:
    - Prolonged heavy drinking leads to alcoholic liver disease, which progresses from fatty liver to alcoholic hepatitis and eventually to cirrhosis.
    - Alcohol metabolism produces harmful substances that damage liver cells, leading to inflammation and fibrosis.

2. **Chronic Viral Hepatitis**:
    - Hepatitis B and C infections can cause chronic inflammation and liver damage, leading to cirrhosis over time.
    - Hepatitis C, in particular, is a significant cause of cirrhosis due to its chronic nature and potential to go undiagnosed for years.

3. **Non-Alcoholic Fatty Liver Disease (NAFLD)**:
    - Associated with obesity, diabetes, and metabolic syndrome, NAFLD can progress to non-alcoholic steatohepatitis (NASH), characterized by inflammation and fibrosis, eventually leading to cirrhosis.

4. **Autoimmune Hepatitis**:
    - The body's immune system attacks liver cells, causing chronic inflammation and damage, leading to cirrhosis.

5. **Genetic Diseases**:

- Conditions such as hemochromatosis (excess iron accumulation) and Wilson's disease (excess copper accumulation) cause liver damage and fibrosis.

6. **Bile Duct Diseases**:
    - Primary biliary cholangitis (PBC) and primary sclerosing cholangitis (PSC) cause inflammation and scarring of the bile ducts, leading to bile buildup and liver damage.

7. **Medications and Toxins**:
    - Long-term use of certain medications, exposure to toxins, and chronic exposure to environmental pollutants can cause liver damage and cirrhosis.

Symptoms

Cirrhosis may not cause noticeable symptoms in its early stages. As the disease progresses, symptoms become more apparent and severe, including:

1. **Fatigue and Weakness**: Persistent tiredness and lack of energy.
2. **Loss of Appetite and Weight Loss**: Reduced desire to eat and unexplained weight loss.
3. **Nausea and Vomiting**: Digestive disturbances, including nausea and vomiting.
4. **Jaundice**: Yellowing of the skin and eyes due to the buildup of bilirubin.
5. **Swelling and Edema**: Fluid retention leading to swelling in the legs, ankles, and abdomen (ascites).
6. **Abdominal Pain**: Discomfort or pain in the upper right quadrant of the abdomen.

7. **Itching**: Generalized itching due to bile salt accumulation.
8. **Bruising and Bleeding**: Easy bruising and bleeding due to impaired liver function affecting blood clotting.
9. **Spider Angiomas**: Small, spider-like blood vessels visible on the skin.
10. **Confusion and Memory Problems**: Hepatic encephalopathy, resulting from toxins building up in the brain.

Diagnosis

Diagnosing cirrhosis involves a combination of medical history, physical examination, laboratory tests, imaging studies, and sometimes liver biopsy:

1. **Medical History**: Evaluation of risk factors such as alcohol consumption, viral hepatitis, and metabolic syndrome.
2. **Physical Examination**: Checking for signs of jaundice, abdominal swelling, spider angiomas, and other physical manifestations of liver disease.
3. **Blood Tests**: Liver function tests (LFTs) to assess levels of liver enzymes (ALT, AST), bilirubin, and albumin. Tests for blood clotting factors (INR) may also be performed.
4. **Imaging Studies**: Ultrasound, CT scan, or MRI to visualize the liver's size, shape, and structure, and to detect signs of fibrosis, nodules, and other abnormalities.
5. **Elastography**: A specialized ultrasound technique that measures liver stiffness, indicating the extent of fibrosis.
6. **Liver Biopsy**: A small tissue sample is taken from the liver and examined under a microscope to confirm the presence and extent of fibrosis and to identify underlying causes.

Treatment Options

Cirrhosis is an irreversible condition, but treatment aims to slow its progression, manage symptoms, and prevent complications. Treatment options include:

1. **Lifestyle Changes**:
    - **Alcohol Abstinence**: Completely avoiding alcohol to prevent further liver damage.
    - **Healthy Diet**: Eating a balanced diet rich in fruits, vegetables, lean proteins, and whole grains. Limiting salt intake to reduce fluid retention.
    - **Regular Exercise**: Engaging in physical activity to maintain a healthy weight and improve overall health.
    - **Avoiding Toxins**: Minimizing exposure to environmental toxins and avoiding unnecessary medications.

2. **Medications**:
    - **Antiviral Drugs**: For hepatitis B or C to reduce viral load and slow liver damage.
    - **Immunosuppressants**: For autoimmune hepatitis to reduce immune-mediated liver damage.
    - **Chelation Therapy**: For genetic conditions like hemochromatosis and Wilson's disease to remove excess iron or copper from the body.

- **Diuretics**: To manage fluid retention and reduce swelling and ascites.
- **Beta-Blockers**: To reduce portal hypertension and prevent variceal bleeding.
- **Lactulose and Rifaximin**: To manage hepatic encephalopathy by reducing toxins in the blood.

3. **Management of Complications**:
    - **Ascites**: Paracentesis to remove excess fluid from the abdomen, and a low-sodium diet to manage fluid retention.
    - **Variceal Bleeding**: Endoscopic procedures to band or sclerose varices, and medications to reduce portal pressure.
    - **Hepatic Encephalopathy**: Medications to reduce ammonia levels and dietary changes to manage symptoms.
    - **Infections**: Prompt treatment of infections with appropriate antibiotics.

4. **Liver Transplant**:
    - For advanced cirrhosis with liver failure, a liver transplant may be the only viable option. Eligibility depends on overall health, severity of liver disease, and other factors.
    - **Evaluation and Listing**: Comprehensive assessment to determine eligibility, followed by listing on the transplant waiting list.
    - **Post-Transplant Care**: Lifelong immunosuppressive therapy to prevent organ rejection and regular monitoring to ensure the transplanted liver's health.

5. **Regular Monitoring**:

- Ongoing medical follow-up to monitor liver function, detect early signs of complications, and adjust treatment as needed.

6. **Supportive Care**:
    - Psychological and social support to help patients cope with the emotional and practical challenges of living with cirrhosis.

Cirrhosis is a serious and progressive liver disease, but with early detection, appropriate medical care, and lifestyle modifications, its progression can be slowed, and complications managed effectively. Understanding the causes, symptoms, diagnosis, and treatment options empowers patients and healthcare providers to take proactive steps in managing this complex condition and improving overall quality of life.

Liver Cancer

Liver cancer, specifically hepatocellular carcinoma (HCC), is a serious and often fatal disease that originates in the liver cells. It's crucial to understand its causes, symptoms, and diagnosis to enable early detection and effective treatment.

Causes

Liver cancer can develop due to several risk factors and underlying conditions that damage the liver. The primary causes include:

1. **Chronic Viral Hepatitis (B and C)**:

- Chronic infection with hepatitis B virus (HBV) or hepatitis C virus (HCV) is one of the most significant risk factors for liver cancer.
- These infections lead to long-term liver inflammation and damage, increasing the likelihood of developing HCC.

2. **Cirrhosis**:
    - Cirrhosis, characterized by extensive scarring of the liver, is a major risk factor for liver cancer.
    - Causes of cirrhosis such as chronic alcohol abuse, NAFLD, and autoimmune diseases contribute to the risk.

3. **Non-Alcoholic Fatty Liver Disease (NAFLD)**:
    - Associated with obesity, diabetes, and metabolic syndrome, NAFLD can progress to non-alcoholic steatohepatitis (NASH) and cirrhosis, increasing the risk of liver cancer.

4. **Chronic Alcohol Abuse**:
    - Long-term heavy alcohol consumption leads to alcoholic liver disease and cirrhosis, significantly raising the risk of liver cancer.

5. **Aflatoxin Exposure**:
    - Aflatoxins are toxic substances produced by certain molds that contaminate crops like peanuts, corn, and grains. Chronic exposure to aflatoxins, particularly in areas with poor food storage practices, is a known risk factor for HCC.

6. **Hemochromatosis**:

- This genetic disorder causes the body to absorb and store too much iron, leading to liver damage and increasing the risk of liver cancer.

7. **Wilson's Disease**:
   - Another genetic disorder where excessive copper accumulation in the liver can lead to damage and increase the risk of liver cancer.

8. **Diabetes**:
   - Type 2 diabetes, especially when associated with obesity, is a risk factor for liver cancer, likely due to its association with NAFLD and metabolic syndrome.

9. **Obesity**:
   - Excess body weight contributes to the development of NAFLD, NASH, and cirrhosis, increasing the risk of liver cancer.

10. **Smoking**:
    - Smoking has been linked to an increased risk of developing liver cancer.

Symptoms

Liver cancer often does not cause symptoms in its early stages. As the disease progresses, symptoms become more apparent and may include:

1. **Unexplained Weight Loss**:
   - Significant and unintentional weight loss is a common symptom.

2. **Loss of Appetite**:

- A reduced desire to eat, often accompanied by a feeling of fullness after small meals.

3. **Upper Abdominal Pain**:
   - Persistent pain or discomfort in the upper right quadrant of the abdomen.

4. **Nausea and Vomiting**:
   - Digestive disturbances, including frequent nausea and vomiting.

5. **General Weakness and Fatigue**:
   - Persistent tiredness and weakness.

6. **Enlarged Liver (Hepatomegaly)**:
   - The liver may feel larger than normal and can be felt as a mass under the ribs on the right side.

7. **Enlarged Spleen (Splenomegaly)**:
   - The spleen may also become enlarged and can be felt as a mass under the ribs on the left side.

8. **Jaundice**:
   - Yellowing of the skin and eyes due to the buildup of bilirubin in the blood.

9. **Dark Urine**:
   - Brownish urine indicating liver dysfunction.

10. **Itching**:
    - Generalized itching due to bile salt accumulation.

11. **Swelling in the Abdomen (Ascites)**:

- Fluid buildup in the abdomen leading to visible swelling.

12. **Fever**:
    - Occasional fever, which may be persistent or intermittent.

Diagnosis

Diagnosing liver cancer involves a combination of medical history, physical examination, laboratory tests, imaging studies, and sometimes biopsy:

1. **Medical History**:
   - Evaluation of risk factors such as chronic hepatitis B or C infection, cirrhosis, alcohol use, and family history of liver cancer.

2. **Physical Examination**:
   - Checking for signs of liver disease such as jaundice, abdominal swelling, and palpable liver or spleen enlargement.

3. **Laboratory Tests**:
   - **Liver Function Tests (LFTs)**: Measuring levels of liver enzymes (ALT, AST), bilirubin, and albumin to assess liver function.
   - **Alpha-Fetoprotein (AFP)**: Elevated levels of AFP, a tumor marker, may indicate liver cancer, although not all liver cancers produce AFP.

4. **Imaging Studies**:

- **Ultrasound**: Often the first imaging test used to detect liver abnormalities and masses.
- **Computed Tomography (CT) Scan**: Provides detailed images of the liver and surrounding structures to identify tumors and assess their size and spread.
- **Magnetic Resonance Imaging (MRI)**: Offers detailed imaging of the liver and helps distinguish between benign and malignant liver lesions.
- **Angiography**: Imaging of blood vessels to assess the blood supply to liver tumors.

5. **Biopsy**:
   - **Liver Biopsy**: A small tissue sample is taken from the liver and examined under a microscope to confirm the presence of cancer cells and determine the type and grade of cancer.

6. **Staging**:
   - Determining the stage of liver cancer is crucial for planning treatment. Staging may involve additional imaging tests and, sometimes, exploratory surgery to assess the extent of cancer spread.

Early detection of liver cancer is challenging due to its asymptomatic nature in the initial stages. Regular screening for high-risk individuals, such as those with chronic hepatitis B or C, cirrhosis, and other risk factors, is essential for early diagnosis and effective treatment. Understanding the causes, symptoms, and diagnostic methods for liver cancer empowers individuals and healthcare providers to take proactive steps in managing this life-threatening condition.

Chapter 3: Causes of Liver Diseases

Lifestyle Factors

The liver is a resilient organ with the ability to regenerate and heal itself, but it is also susceptible to damage from various lifestyle factors. These factors can significantly impact liver health and contribute to the development of liver diseases. Understanding how diet, alcohol consumption, obesity, and physical inactivity influence liver health is crucial for preventing and managing liver diseases.

Diet and Nutrition

Diet and nutrition play a pivotal role in maintaining liver health. Poor dietary choices can lead to various liver conditions, including non-alcoholic fatty liver disease (NAFLD), which is one of the most common liver diseases worldwide.

1. **High-Fat Diets:**
    - Diets rich in saturated fats and trans fats can contribute to the accumulation of fat in liver cells, leading to fatty liver

disease. Foods like fast food, fried items, and processed snacks are typical culprits.

2. **High-Sugar Diets**:
   - Excessive consumption of sugar, particularly fructose found in sugary beverages and processed foods, can lead to fat buildup in the liver. This condition, known as non-alcoholic fatty liver disease (NAFLD), can progress to more severe liver damage.

3. **High-Calorie Diets**:
   - Consistently consuming more calories than the body needs can result in weight gain and obesity, which are significant risk factors for NAFLD and other liver diseases.

4. **Low Fiber Intake**:
   - A diet low in fiber, which is found in fruits, vegetables, whole grains, and legumes, can contribute to poor liver health. Fiber helps regulate blood sugar levels and supports overall metabolic health.

5. **Micronutrient Deficiencies**:
   - Deficiencies in essential vitamins and minerals, such as vitamin D, vitamin E, and omega-3 fatty acids, can negatively affect liver function and increase the risk of liver disease.

Alcohol Consumption

Alcohol consumption is a well-known cause of liver disease, with heavy and prolonged drinking leading to a range of liver conditions.

1. **Alcoholic Fatty Liver Disease**:
   - This is the earliest stage of alcohol-related liver disease, characterized by fat accumulation in liver cells due to excessive alcohol intake. While it is usually reversible with abstinence, continued drinking can lead to more severe liver damage.

2. **Alcoholic Hepatitis**:
   - Prolonged heavy drinking can cause inflammation and damage to liver cells, leading to alcoholic hepatitis. Symptoms include jaundice, abdominal pain, and fever. Severe cases can be life-threatening and require immediate medical attention.

3. **Alcoholic Cirrhosis**:
   - Chronic alcohol abuse can result in cirrhosis, a condition where healthy liver tissue is replaced with scar tissue. Cirrhosis impairs liver function and can lead to liver failure. It is often irreversible, but stopping alcohol consumption can prevent further damage.

4. **Increased Susceptibility to Other Liver Diseases**:
   - Alcohol can weaken the liver's defenses, making it more susceptible to viral infections such as hepatitis B and C, which can further exacerbate liver damage.

Obesity

Obesity is a significant risk factor for various liver diseases, particularly non-alcoholic fatty liver disease (NAFLD).

1. **Fat Accumulation in the Liver**:
    - Obesity leads to the accumulation of excess fat in liver cells, a condition known as hepatic steatosis or fatty liver. This can progress to non-alcoholic steatohepatitis (NASH), which involves liver inflammation and damage.
2. **Insulin Resistance and Metabolic Syndrome**:
    - Obesity is often associated with insulin resistance and metabolic syndrome, which include a cluster of conditions such as high blood pressure, high blood sugar, and abnormal cholesterol levels. These conditions can contribute to liver inflammation and fibrosis.
3. **Progression to Cirrhosis and Liver Cancer**:
    - In severe cases, NAFLD and NASH can progress to cirrhosis and increase the risk of developing hepatocellular carcinoma (HCC), a type of liver cancer.
4. **Impact on Other Liver Conditions**:
    - Obesity can worsen the prognosis of other liver diseases, such as viral hepatitis and alcoholic liver disease, by accelerating liver damage and fibrosis.

Physical Inactivity

A sedentary lifestyle and lack of physical activity are major contributors to poor liver health. Regular exercise is essential for maintaining a healthy liver and preventing liver diseases.

1. **Contribution to Obesity**:

- Physical inactivity contributes to weight gain and obesity, which are major risk factors for NAFLD and other liver diseases.

2. **Insulin Resistance**:
    - Regular physical activity helps improve insulin sensitivity, reducing the risk of insulin resistance and metabolic syndrome, both of which are linked to liver disease.

3. **Reduction of Inflammation**:
    - Exercise has anti-inflammatory effects that can help reduce liver inflammation and prevent the progression of liver diseases such as NASH.

4. **Improvement in Liver Enzyme Levels**:
    - Studies have shown that regular physical activity can lead to improvements in liver enzyme levels, indicating better liver function.

5. **Enhanced Metabolic Health**:
    - Physical activity supports overall metabolic health, including better regulation of blood sugar and lipid levels, which are crucial for preventing liver disease.

In conclusion, lifestyle factors play a crucial role in the development and progression of liver diseases. Maintaining a healthy diet, limiting alcohol consumption, managing body weight, and engaging in regular physical activity are essential strategies for protecting liver health. By making informed lifestyle choices, individuals can significantly reduce their risk of liver disease and promote long-term liver health.

Environmental Factors

Environmental factors significantly contribute to liver diseases, often through exposure to toxins, chemicals, and viral infections. These factors can cause acute liver damage or lead to chronic conditions that progressively impair liver function.

Toxins and Chemicals

Exposure to various toxins and chemicals in the environment can cause significant liver damage. These substances can be encountered in occupational settings, through contaminated food and water, or as a result of pollution.

1. **Industrial Chemicals**:
    - **Solvents**: Organic solvents such as carbon tetrachloride, chloroform, and vinyl chloride, commonly used in industrial processes, can cause acute and chronic liver damage.
    - **Pesticides and Herbicides**: Exposure to certain pesticides and herbicides can lead to toxic liver injury. These chemicals can accumulate in the liver, causing inflammation, fibrosis, and eventually cirrhosis.
2. **Heavy Metals**:
    - **Lead**: Chronic exposure to lead, often found in old paints, contaminated soil, and industrial emissions, can cause liver toxicity.

- o **Mercury**: Exposure to mercury, found in some industrial processes and contaminated fish, can lead to liver damage.
- o **Arsenic**: Chronic exposure to arsenic, found in contaminated water and certain pesticides, can cause liver fibrosis and cirrhosis.

3. **Mycotoxins**:
   - o **Aflatoxins**: Produced by certain molds (Aspergillus species), aflatoxins can contaminate crops like peanuts, corn, and grains. Chronic exposure to aflatoxins is a significant risk factor for hepatocellular carcinoma (HCC).

4. **Environmental Pollutants**:
   - o **Air Pollution**: Exposure to air pollutants such as particulate matter, sulfur dioxide, and nitrogen oxides can contribute to liver inflammation and fibrosis.
   - o **Water Contaminants**: Contaminants in water, including industrial runoff, heavy metals, and agricultural chemicals, can cause liver toxicity.

5. **Medications and Drugs**:
   - o **Acetaminophen (Paracetamol)**: Overdose or chronic use of acetaminophen is a common cause of acute liver failure.
   - o **Prescription Medications**: Certain medications, including statins, antiepileptic drugs, and some antibiotics, can cause liver damage as a side effect.
   - o **Illicit Drugs**: Drugs such as cocaine and ecstasy can cause acute liver injury and chronic damage with long-term use.

Viral Infections

Viral infections are a major cause of liver diseases worldwide, leading to both acute and chronic conditions that can result in severe liver damage.

1. **Hepatitis A**:
    - **Causes**: Hepatitis A virus (HAV) is primarily transmitted through the ingestion of contaminated food or water.
    - **Symptoms**: Symptoms include fever, fatigue, nausea, vomiting, abdominal pain, jaundice, and dark urine.
    - **Diagnosis**: Diagnosis is typically made through blood tests that detect HAV antibodies.
    - **Prevention**: Vaccination is the most effective way to prevent hepatitis A. Improved sanitation and safe food and water practices also reduce the risk.

2. **Hepatitis B**:
    - **Causes**: Hepatitis B virus (HBV) is transmitted through contact with infected blood or body fluids, including sexual contact, sharing needles, and from mother to child during childbirth.
    - **Symptoms**: Acute HBV infection may cause jaundice, fatigue, abdominal pain, and flu-like symptoms. Chronic HBV infection can lead to cirrhosis and liver cancer.
    - **Diagnosis**: Blood tests detect HBV antigens and antibodies. Chronic infection is monitored through liver function tests and viral load measurements.
    - **Prevention**: Vaccination is highly effective in preventing HBV infection. Safe practices, such as using clean needles and practicing safe sex, also reduce transmission risk.

3. **Hepatitis C**:

- **Causes**: Hepatitis C virus (HCV) is primarily transmitted through blood-to-blood contact, such as sharing needles and through contaminated medical equipment. It can also be transmitted sexually or from mother to child.
- **Symptoms**: Acute HCV infection is often asymptomatic. Chronic HCV infection can lead to cirrhosis, liver failure, and liver cancer.
- **Diagnosis**: Blood tests detect HCV antibodies and viral RNA. Liver biopsy or imaging may be used to assess liver damage.
- **Prevention**: There is no vaccine for HCV. Prevention includes avoiding sharing needles, ensuring safe medical practices, and practicing safe sex.

4. **Hepatitis D**:
   - **Causes**: Hepatitis D virus (HDV) requires the presence of HBV to replicate and is transmitted through similar routes (blood and body fluids).
   - **Symptoms**: Co-infection or superinfection with HDV can cause more severe liver disease than HBV alone.
   - **Diagnosis**: Blood tests detect HDV antibodies and RNA.
   - **Prevention**: Preventing HBV infection through vaccination also prevents HDV infection. Safe practices to avoid HBV transmission apply.

5. **Hepatitis E**:
   - **Causes**: Hepatitis E virus (HEV) is transmitted primarily through the ingestion of contaminated water.

- **Symptoms**: Symptoms are similar to hepatitis A, including jaundice, fatigue, abdominal pain, and nausea.
- **Diagnosis**: Blood tests detect HEV antibodies and RNA.
- **Prevention**: Ensuring access to clean water and improved sanitation are key preventive measures. Vaccines are available in some regions.

6. **Other Viral Infections**:
    - **Cytomegalovirus (CMV)**: CMV can cause liver inflammation, particularly in immunocompromised individuals.
    - **Epstein-Barr Virus (EBV)**: EBV infection can lead to liver inflammation and hepatitis, particularly in young adults.

In conclusion, environmental factors, including exposure to toxins, chemicals, and viral infections, play a significant role in the development of liver diseases. Understanding these factors and implementing preventive measures can help reduce the risk of liver damage and promote liver health. This highlights the importance of public health initiatives, safe practices, and early detection strategies in managing and preventing liver diseases caused by environmental factors.

Genetic Factors

Genetic factors play a crucial role in the development of various liver diseases. Inherited genetic mutations and hereditary conditions can lead to abnormal liver function, liver damage, and an increased risk of chronic liver diseases. Understanding these genetic factors helps in early diagnosis, management, and potentially in preventive strategies for individuals with a family history of liver disease or those carrying specific genetic mutations.

Genetic Disorders Leading to Liver Disease

1. **Hemochromatosis**:
   - **Overview**: Hemochromatosis is an inherited condition characterized by excessive iron accumulation in the body, particularly in the liver. This excess iron leads to oxidative stress, inflammation, and eventually fibrosis and cirrhosis.
   - **Causes**: The most common genetic mutation associated with hemochromatosis is in the HFE gene. Mutations such as C282Y and H63D disrupt normal iron absorption and regulation.
   - **Symptoms**: Symptoms may include joint pain, diabetes, skin discoloration (bronze or gray), fatigue, and abdominal pain. If left untreated, it can progress to liver cirrhosis and liver cancer.
   - **Diagnosis**: Diagnosis involves blood tests to measure serum ferritin and transferrin saturation levels, genetic testing for HFE mutations, and liver biopsy to assess the extent of iron deposition and liver damage.
   - **Treatment**: Treatment primarily involves regular phlebotomy (blood removal) to reduce iron levels, along with dietary modifications and monitoring for complications.

2. **Wilson's Disease**:
   - **Overview**: Wilson's disease is a genetic disorder that leads to abnormal copper accumulation in the liver and other tissues. This copper buildup results in liver damage, neurological symptoms, and psychiatric issues.

- **Causes**: The condition is caused by mutations in the ATP7B gene, which impairs copper transport and excretion.

- **Symptoms**: Symptoms can include liver dysfunction, jaundice, abdominal pain, tremors, dysarthria, psychiatric disturbances, and motor abnormalities. Without treatment, Wilson's disease can lead to liver failure and neurological deterioration.

- **Diagnosis**: Diagnosis involves measuring copper levels in the blood and urine, liver biopsy to assess copper accumulation, and genetic testing for ATP7B mutations.

- **Treatment**: Treatment includes chelating agents (such as penicillamine or trientine) that help remove excess copper, along with zinc supplements to reduce copper absorption. Lifelong management is required to prevent copper buildup.

3. **Alpha-1 Antitrypsin Deficiency**:

    - **Overview**: Alpha-1 antitrypsin (AAT) deficiency is a genetic disorder that leads to low levels of the AAT protein, which protects the liver and lungs from damage. The deficiency results in liver disease and emphysema.

    - **Causes**: Mutations in the SERPINA1 gene affect the production and secretion of AAT protein. The most common variant associated with the deficiency is the Z allele.

    - **Symptoms**: Symptoms can include liver disease in childhood or adulthood, jaundice, abdominal pain, chronic obstructive pulmonary disease (COPD), and emphysema.

- **Diagnosis**: Diagnosis involves blood tests to measure AAT levels, genetic testing for SERPINA1 mutations, and liver biopsy to assess liver damage.
- **Treatment**: Treatment includes managing symptoms and complications, such as liver transplantation for severe liver disease and augmentation therapy with AAT protein replacement.

4. **Cystic Fibrosis**:
   - **Overview**: Cystic fibrosis (CF) is a genetic disorder affecting multiple organs, including the liver. The disorder leads to thick, sticky mucus production, which can cause liver damage and bile duct obstruction.
   - **Causes**: CF is caused by mutations in the CFTR gene, leading to defective chloride channels and abnormal mucus production.
   - **Symptoms**: Liver symptoms may include jaundice, abdominal pain, pruritus (itching), and liver fibrosis. CF also affects the lungs, pancreas, and digestive system.
   - **Diagnosis**: Diagnosis involves sweat chloride testing, genetic testing for CFTR mutations, and imaging studies to assess liver involvement.
   - **Treatment**: Treatment focuses on managing symptoms and complications, including enzyme replacement therapy, medications to thin mucus, and liver transplantation for severe liver damage.

5. **Familial Hypercholesterolemia**:
   - **Overview**: Familial hypercholesterolemia is a genetic disorder characterized by high levels of cholesterol in the

blood, which can lead to the development of atherosclerosis and liver disease.

- **Causes**: The condition is caused by mutations in genes such as LDLR (low-density lipoprotein receptor), APOB (apolipoprotein B), or PCSK9 (proprotein convertase subtilisin/kexin type 9), affecting cholesterol metabolism.
- **Symptoms**: Symptoms include elevated cholesterol levels, xanthomas (cholesterol deposits in the skin), and an increased risk of cardiovascular disease. Liver symptoms may include fatty liver disease.
- **Diagnosis**: Diagnosis involves blood tests to measure cholesterol levels, genetic testing for mutations, and imaging studies to assess liver involvement.
- **Treatment**: Treatment includes cholesterol-lowering medications (such as statins), lifestyle modifications, and monitoring for cardiovascular and liver complications.

Genetic Predisposition to Liver Cancer

Certain genetic predispositions can increase the risk of developing liver cancer, often in the context of chronic liver diseases. For example:

1. **Genetic Variants**: Some genetic variants may increase susceptibility to liver cancer in individuals with chronic hepatitis B or C infection, cirrhosis, or NAFLD.
2. **Family History**: A family history of liver cancer can indicate a genetic predisposition to the disease, highlighting the need for regular screening and early intervention.

Genetic factors contribute significantly to liver diseases through inherited mutations and genetic disorders. Conditions such as hemochromatosis, Wilson's disease, alpha-1 antitrypsin deficiency, cystic fibrosis, and familial hypercholesterolemia highlight the impact of genetic abnormalities on liver health. Early diagnosis through genetic testing and family history assessment, along with appropriate management and treatment, can help mitigate the effects of these genetic disorders and improve outcomes for affected individuals. Understanding these genetic factors is crucial for preventive measures, early intervention, and effective management of liver diseases.

Other Health Conditions

In addition to lifestyle factors, environmental exposures, and genetic predispositions, various other health conditions can significantly impact liver health. These conditions can either directly affect the liver or exacerbate existing liver diseases. Understanding these health conditions is crucial for the prevention, diagnosis, and management of liver diseases.

1. Diabetes Mellitus

Overview: Diabetes mellitus, particularly type 2 diabetes, is a chronic condition characterized by high blood sugar levels resulting from insulin resistance or inadequate insulin production. Diabetes is closely linked to liver diseases due to its impact on metabolism and fat accumulation.

Impact on Liver Health:

- **Non-Alcoholic Fatty Liver Disease (NAFLD)**: Diabetes increases the risk of developing NAFLD, a condition where excess fat accumulates in liver cells without alcohol consumption. NAFLD can progress to non-alcoholic steatohepatitis (NASH) and eventually to cirrhosis and liver cancer.

- **Insulin Resistance**: Insulin resistance, a hallmark of type 2 diabetes, is associated with increased fat deposition in the liver and liver inflammation.
- **Increased Risk of Fibrosis**: Chronic high blood sugar levels can exacerbate liver fibrosis and progression of liver disease.

Management: Controlling blood sugar levels through diet, medication, and lifestyle changes is essential for managing diabetes and reducing its impact on liver health. Regular monitoring and treatment of NAFLD and associated liver conditions are also crucial.

2. Hypertension (High Blood Pressure)

Overview: Hypertension is a condition characterized by elevated blood pressure levels. Chronic high blood pressure can lead to damage to various organs, including the liver.

Impact on Liver Health:

- **Portal Hypertension**: One of the significant complications of chronic liver disease is portal hypertension, where increased blood pressure in the portal vein (which supplies blood to the liver) occurs. This condition can result from cirrhosis or other chronic liver diseases and can lead to complications such as variceal bleeding.
- **Liver Fibrosis**: Chronic hypertension can contribute to liver fibrosis by increasing the pressure within the liver's blood vessels and exacerbating liver damage.

Management: Managing hypertension through lifestyle changes, medication, and monitoring can help prevent liver complications associated with high blood pressure.

3. Chronic Kidney Disease (CKD)

Overview: Chronic kidney disease is a progressive condition where kidney function declines over time. CKD can have a significant impact on liver health due to fluid and waste buildup in the body.

Impact on Liver Health:

- **Hepatorenal Syndrome**: In advanced stages of liver disease, kidney dysfunction may occur, leading to hepatorenal syndrome, a serious complication characterized by rapid kidney failure in the context of severe liver disease.

- **Increased Risk of Liver Disease Progression**: CKD can exacerbate liver disease progression by affecting metabolic processes and fluid balance.

Management: Managing CKD involves controlling underlying causes such as diabetes and hypertension, monitoring kidney function, and considering liver and kidney function together in treatment plans.

4. Autoimmune Disorders

Overview: Autoimmune disorders occur when the immune system mistakenly attacks the body's own tissues. Several autoimmune conditions can affect the liver, leading to inflammation and damage.

Impact on Liver Health:

- **Autoimmune Hepatitis**: A chronic condition where the immune system attacks liver cells, causing inflammation, liver damage, and potentially cirrhosis. Symptoms can include jaundice, fatigue, and abdominal pain.

- **Primary Biliary Cholangitis (PBC)**: An autoimmune disorder that damages and destroys the bile ducts within the liver, leading to bile accumulation, liver inflammation, and fibrosis.
- **Primary Sclerosing Cholangitis (PSC)**: An autoimmune condition characterized by inflammation and scarring of the bile ducts, which can lead to liver damage and increase the risk of liver cancer.

Management: Treatment involves immunosuppressive medications, managing symptoms, and monitoring liver function to slow disease progression and prevent complications.

5. Hyperlipidemia

Overview: Hyperlipidemia refers to elevated levels of lipids (fats) in the blood, including cholesterol and triglycerides. This condition can contribute to liver damage through its effects on fat metabolism.

Impact on Liver Health:

- **Non-Alcoholic Fatty Liver Disease (NAFLD)**: Elevated lipid levels can lead to fat accumulation in liver cells, contributing to NAFLD, which can progress to NASH and cirrhosis.
- **Increased Risk of Atherosclerosis**: Hyperlipidemia can exacerbate liver damage by promoting atherosclerosis, which affects blood flow and can contribute to liver disease complications.

Management: Managing hyperlipidemia involves lifestyle modifications such as diet and exercise, along with medications to lower lipid levels and reduce the risk of liver disease.

6. Inflammatory Bowel Disease (IBD)

Overview: Inflammatory bowel disease, including Crohn's disease and ulcerative colitis, involves chronic inflammation of the digestive tract and can affect liver health.

Impact on Liver Health:

- **Primary Sclerosing Cholangitis (PSC)**: PSC is a condition that often occurs in individuals with IBD, leading to inflammation and scarring of the bile ducts and an increased risk of liver damage and cancer.
- **Liver Dysfunction**: Chronic inflammation and medications used to treat IBD can affect liver function and contribute to liver disease.

Management: Managing IBD through medications, dietary adjustments, and monitoring liver function is essential to prevent liver complications and improve overall health.

7. Thyroid Disorders

Overview: Thyroid disorders, including hypothyroidism (underactive thyroid) and hyperthyroidism (overactive thyroid), can influence liver health due to their impact on metabolism and hormonal balance.

Impact on Liver Health:

- **Hypothyroidism**: Can lead to elevated cholesterol levels and liver enzyme abnormalities. Chronic hypothyroidism may contribute to NAFLD and liver dysfunction.
- **Hyperthyroidism**: Can cause increased liver enzyme levels and may affect liver function through its impact on metabolism and cardiovascular health.

Management: Treating thyroid disorders with appropriate medication and monitoring thyroid function can help manage its effects on liver health and prevent complications.

Various health conditions can significantly impact liver health, either by directly affecting liver function or by exacerbating existing liver diseases. Diabetes mellitus, hypertension, chronic kidney disease, autoimmune disorders, hyperlipidemia, inflammatory bowel disease, and thyroid disorders are among the conditions that can contribute to liver damage. Proper management of these conditions through lifestyle changes, medication, and regular monitoring is essential for preventing liver complications and maintaining overall health. Understanding the interplay between these health conditions and liver disease is crucial for effective treatment and prevention strategies.

Chapter 4: Prevention and Solutions for Common Liver Diseases

Dietary Changes

Dietary changes are fundamental in managing and preventing common liver diseases. The liver plays a crucial role in metabolizing nutrients, detoxifying harmful substances, and storing energy. Adopting a liver-friendly diet can help reduce inflammation, prevent fat accumulation, and support overall liver health.

1. **Balanced Diet**:
    - **Nutrient-Rich Foods**: Incorporate a variety of fruits, vegetables, whole grains, and lean proteins. These foods provide essential vitamins, minerals, and antioxidants that support liver function and repair.
    - **Healthy Fats**: Opt for sources of unsaturated fats, such as olive oil, avocados, and nuts, which can help reduce liver fat and inflammation. Avoid trans fats and limit saturated fats found in processed foods and fatty cuts of meat.

2. **Reduced Sugar Intake**:
    - **Limit Added Sugars**: Excessive consumption of sugar, particularly fructose, can contribute to fat buildup in the liver. Minimize intake of sugary beverages, desserts, and processed snacks.
    - **Whole Foods**: Choose whole grains and fruits with natural sugars over refined and processed options to help maintain balanced blood sugar levels and reduce liver fat.

3. **Moderation in Protein Consumption**:
    - **Lean Proteins**: Incorporate lean protein sources like fish, chicken, beans, and legumes. High-quality protein supports liver repair and function without contributing to excess fat accumulation.

- **Portion Control**: Avoid excessive protein intake, which can put additional strain on the liver, especially in individuals with pre-existing liver conditions.

4. **Adequate Hydration**:
    - **Water Intake**: Drink plenty of water throughout the day to support liver detoxification processes and maintain proper hydration.
    - **Limit Alcohol and Caffeine**: Reduce consumption of alcoholic beverages and excessive caffeine, as these can stress the liver and contribute to liver disease progression.

5. **Specific Dietary Approaches**:
    - **Mediterranean Diet**: Emphasize a Mediterranean diet rich in fruits, vegetables, whole grains, lean proteins, and healthy fats, which has been shown to benefit liver health and reduce the risk of liver disease.
    - **Anti-Inflammatory Foods**: Include foods with anti-inflammatory properties, such as turmeric, ginger, garlic, and green tea, to help reduce liver inflammation and support overall liver health.

Lifestyle Modifications

Lifestyle modifications play a crucial role in the prevention and management of liver diseases. Implementing positive changes in daily habits can significantly impact liver health and reduce the risk of liver-related conditions.

1. **Regular Physical Activity**:
   - **Exercise Routine**: Engage in regular physical activity, including aerobic exercises (e.g., walking, running, cycling) and strength training. Aim for at least 150 minutes of moderate-intensity exercise per week.
   - **Weight Management**: Exercise helps maintain a healthy weight and reduces fat accumulation in the liver, which is particularly important for preventing and managing non-alcoholic fatty liver disease (NAFLD).

2. **Weight Management**:
   - **Healthy Weight**: Achieve and maintain a healthy weight through a combination of balanced diet and regular exercise. Excess body weight is a major risk factor for liver diseases, including NAFLD and cirrhosis.
   - **Gradual Weight Loss**: For individuals who are overweight or obese, aim for gradual weight loss (1-2 pounds per week) to avoid rapid changes that can stress the liver.

3. **Avoiding Alcohol and Tobacco**:
   - **Alcohol Limitation**: Limit alcohol consumption or abstain entirely, especially if there is a history of liver disease. Excessive alcohol intake can lead to liver inflammation, fatty liver, and cirrhosis.
   - **Quit Smoking**: Avoid tobacco products, as smoking can exacerbate liver damage and increase the risk of liver cancer. Seek support and resources to quit smoking.

4. **Stress Management**:
   - **Relaxation Techniques**: Incorporate stress-reducing practices such as mindfulness, meditation, yoga, and deep-

breathing exercises. Chronic stress can negatively impact liver health and contribute to inflammation.
- **Healthy Sleep**: Prioritize good sleep hygiene to ensure adequate rest and recovery. Poor sleep patterns can affect metabolic health and liver function.

5. **Safe Practices**:
   - **Avoiding Drug Abuse**: Avoid illicit drug use and misuse of prescription medications, which can lead to liver toxicity and damage.
   - **Safe Medical Practices**: Use safe medical practices, including ensuring sterile conditions during medical procedures and avoiding sharing needles to prevent viral hepatitis.

Medical Treatments

Medical treatments are essential for managing and treating liver diseases, especially when lifestyle modifications and dietary changes alone are not sufficient.

1. **Medications**:
   - **Antiviral Medications**: For viral hepatitis (e.g., hepatitis B and C), antiviral medications can help reduce viral load, prevent liver damage, and improve liver function.
   - **Anti-Inflammatory Drugs**: In conditions such as autoimmune hepatitis, anti-inflammatory and immunosuppressive drugs are used to reduce liver inflammation and prevent further damage.

- **Medications for NAFLD/NASH**: Although no specific medications are approved for NAFLD or NASH, certain medications such as vitamin E and medications targeting insulin resistance may be used to manage symptoms.

2. **Hormonal Treatments**:
   - **Estrogen Therapy**: In some cases, hormonal treatments may be used to manage liver conditions associated with hormonal imbalances, such as primary biliary cholangitis (PBC).

3. **Surgical Interventions**:
   - **Liver Biopsy**: A liver biopsy may be performed to assess the extent of liver damage and guide treatment decisions.
   - **Liver Transplantation**: For individuals with advanced liver disease or cirrhosis, liver transplantation may be necessary. This procedure involves replacing the damaged liver with a healthy donor liver.

4. **Specialized Therapies**:
   - **Chelation Therapy**: For conditions such as Wilson's disease, chelation therapy is used to remove excess copper from the body and prevent liver damage.
   - **Phlebotomy**: In hemochromatosis, regular phlebotomy is performed to reduce excess iron levels and prevent liver damage.

Regular Monitoring and Check-Ups

Regular monitoring and check-ups are crucial for the early detection, management, and prevention of liver diseases. Routine evaluations help assess liver function, track disease progression, and adjust treatment plans as needed.

1. **Routine Liver Function Tests**:
   - **Blood Tests**: Regular liver function tests (LFTs) measure levels of liver enzymes, bilirubin, and other indicators of liver health. Elevated levels can signal liver damage or disease.
   - **Screening for Liver Disease**: For individuals at risk of liver disease (e.g., those with a family history or chronic conditions), regular screening tests, such as hepatitis virus tests and imaging studies, are essential.

2. **Imaging Studies**:
   - **Ultrasound**: Liver ultrasound is commonly used to assess liver size, structure, and the presence of abnormalities such as fatty liver or tumors.
   - **CT and MRI Scans**: Advanced imaging techniques, such as computed tomography (CT) and magnetic resonance imaging (MRI), may be used for detailed evaluation of liver conditions and detecting complications.

3. **Follow-Up Appointments**:
   - **Specialist Visits**: Regular visits to a hepatologist or gastroenterologist are important for monitoring liver health and adjusting treatment plans as needed.
   - **Management of Comorbidities**: Ongoing management of associated conditions, such as diabetes and hypertension, is crucial for overall liver health and disease prevention.

4. **Patient Education and Support**:

- **Lifestyle Counseling**: Educating patients about lifestyle changes, dietary modifications, and medication adherence helps improve outcomes and prevent disease progression.

- **Support Groups**: Participation in support groups for individuals with liver diseases can provide emotional support and practical advice for managing chronic conditions.

In conclusion, addressing liver health through dietary changes, lifestyle modifications, medical treatments, and regular monitoring is essential for preventing and managing common liver diseases. By making informed decisions and following a comprehensive approach, individuals can significantly improve liver health, prevent disease progression, and enhance overall quality of life.

Chapter 5: Liver-Friendly Breakfast Recipes

Starting your day with liver-friendly breakfast options can set a positive tone for your overall health. These recipes focus on incorporating ingredients that support liver function, reduce inflammation, and promote overall well-being. Here's an extensive guide to liver-friendly breakfast options:

Smoothie Bowls

Overview: Smoothie bowls are a versatile and nutritious breakfast option. They can be customized with a variety of fruits, vegetables, and healthy toppings, providing essential vitamins and minerals beneficial for liver health.

Recipe 1: Berry Spinach Smoothie Bowl

- **Ingredients**:
    - 1 cup fresh spinach
    - 1 cup mixed berries (blueberries, strawberries, raspberries)
    - 1/2 banana
    - 1/2 cup unsweetened almond milk (or other plant-based milk)
    - 1 tablespoon chia seeds
    - 1 teaspoon flaxseeds
    - Toppings: sliced strawberries, granola, hemp seeds, a few mint leaves

- **Instructions**:

1. Blend the spinach, mixed berries, banana, and almond milk until smooth.
2. Pour the smoothie into a bowl.
3. Sprinkle with chia seeds, flaxseeds, and your choice of toppings.
4. Serve immediately.

- **Benefits**: Spinach and berries are rich in antioxidants and fiber, which help reduce inflammation and support liver health. Chia and flaxseeds add omega-3 fatty acids and fiber, promoting overall wellness.

Recipe 2: Tropical Green Smoothie Bowl

- **Ingredients**:
    - 1 cup kale or spinach
    - 1/2 cup pineapple chunks (fresh or frozen)
    - 1/2 cup mango chunks (fresh or frozen)
    - 1/2 avocado
    - 1/2 cup coconut water
    - 1 tablespoon pumpkin seeds
    - Toppings: diced mango, coconut flakes, a handful of granola
- **Instructions**:

1. Blend kale, pineapple, mango, avocado, and coconut water until smooth.
2. Pour into a bowl and top with pumpkin seeds, diced mango, coconut flakes, and granola.

3. Enjoy right away.

- **Benefits**: Pineapple and mango provide vitamins A and C, while kale and avocado offer antioxidants and healthy fats. Coconut water helps with hydration.

Oatmeal Variations

Overview: Oatmeal is a hearty and versatile breakfast option. It's rich in fiber, which supports liver function and helps maintain a healthy weight.

Recipe 1: Apple Cinnamon Oatmeal

- **Ingredients**:
    - 1 cup rolled oats
    - 2 cups water or unsweetened almond milk
    - 1 apple, diced
    - 1 teaspoon ground cinnamon
    - 1 tablespoon walnuts, chopped
    - 1 tablespoon maple syrup or honey (optional)
- **Instructions**:

1. In a pot, combine oats and water or almond milk. Bring to a boil, then reduce heat and simmer for 5 minutes.

2. Add diced apple and cinnamon, stirring occasionally until oats are tender and apple is softened.

3. Top with walnuts and a drizzle of maple syrup or honey if desired.

- **Benefits**: Apples provide fiber and antioxidants, while cinnamon helps regulate blood sugar levels. Walnuts add healthy fats, supporting overall liver health.

Recipe 2: Berry Almond Oatmeal

- **Ingredients**:
    - 1 cup steel-cut oats
    - 3 cups water or unsweetened almond milk
    - 1/2 cup mixed berries (fresh or frozen)
    - 2 tablespoons sliced almonds
    - 1 tablespoon flaxseeds
    - 1 teaspoon vanilla extract (optional)
- **Instructions**:

1. Combine oats and water or almond milk in a pot and bring to a boil. Reduce heat and simmer for 20-25 minutes, stirring occasionally.

2. Stir in berries and vanilla extract, cooking for an additional 5 minutes.

3. Serve topped with sliced almonds and flaxseeds.

- **Benefits**: Mixed berries offer antioxidants and vitamins, while flaxseeds provide omega-3 fatty acids and fiber. Almonds add crunch and healthy fats.

Liver-Friendly Pancakes

Overview: Pancakes can be made liver-friendly by using whole grains, healthy fats, and avoiding excessive sugar.

Recipe 1: Whole Wheat Banana Pancakes

- **Ingredients**:
    - 1 cup whole wheat flour
    - 1 tablespoon baking powder
    - 1/2 teaspoon salt
    - 1 cup unsweetened almond milk
    - 1 ripe banana, mashed
    - 1 teaspoon vanilla extract
    - 1 tablespoon coconut oil (for cooking)
- **Instructions**:

1. In a bowl, mix whole wheat flour, baking powder, and salt.

2. In another bowl, combine almond milk, mashed banana, and vanilla extract.

3. Gradually add the wet ingredients to the dry ingredients, stirring until just combined.

4. Heat coconut oil in a skillet over medium heat. Pour batter onto the skillet, cooking until bubbles form and the edges look dry. Flip and cook until golden brown.

- **Benefits**: Whole wheat flour adds fiber and nutrients, while banana provides natural sweetness and potassium. Coconut oil is a healthy fat choice.

Recipe 2: Oatmeal Pancakes

- **Ingredients:**
    - 1 cup rolled oats
    - 1/2 cup almond flour
    - 1 tablespoon baking powder
    - 1/2 teaspoon cinnamon
    - 1 cup unsweetened almond milk
    - 2 eggs
    - 1 tablespoon honey or maple syrup (optional)
- **Instructions:**

1. Blend oats in a food processor until they reach a fine flour consistency.

2. In a bowl, mix oat flour, almond flour, baking powder, and cinnamon.

3. In another bowl, whisk together almond milk, eggs, and honey or maple syrup.

4. Combine wet and dry ingredients until smooth.

5. Heat a non-stick skillet over medium heat and cook pancakes until bubbles form, then flip and cook until golden brown.

- **Benefits:** Oatmeal provides fiber and almond flour adds protein. These pancakes are low in sugar and rich in nutrients.

Egg-Based Dishes

Overview: Eggs are a great source of high-quality protein and essential nutrients. Liver-friendly egg dishes can be made with vegetables and healthy fats.

Recipe 1: Veggie-Stuffed Omelette

- **Ingredients**:
    - 3 eggs
    - 1/4 cup chopped spinach
    - 1/4 cup diced bell peppers
    - 1/4 cup mushrooms, sliced
    - 1 tablespoon olive oil
    - Salt and pepper to taste
- **Instructions**:

1. Heat olive oil in a non-stick skillet over medium heat.
2. Add mushrooms, bell peppers, and spinach, cooking until vegetables are tender.
3. Beat eggs in a bowl and pour over the vegetables.
4. Cook until eggs are set, then fold the omelette in half and serve.

- **Benefits**: Spinach and bell peppers are rich in antioxidants and vitamins, while eggs provide high-quality protein and healthy fats.

Recipe 2: Smoked Salmon and Avocado Egg Scramble

- **Ingredients**:
    - 3 eggs
    - 1/4 cup diced smoked salmon
    - 1/4 avocado, sliced
    - 1 tablespoon chives, chopped
    - 1 tablespoon olive oil
    - Salt and pepper to taste
- **Instructions**:

1. Heat olive oil in a skillet over medium heat.
2. Scramble eggs in the skillet, stirring gently.
3. Add smoked salmon and cook until eggs are fully set.
4. Serve with avocado slices and chopped chives on top.

- **Benefits**: Smoked salmon provides omega-3 fatty acids, and avocado adds healthy fats, supporting liver health and overall wellness.

Whole Grain Toasts

Overview: Whole grain toasts offer fiber and essential nutrients. They can be topped with various liver-friendly ingredients for a satisfying breakfast.

Recipe 1: Avocado Toast with Cherry Tomatoes

- **Ingredients**:
    - 1 slice whole grain bread

- 1/2 avocado
- 1/4 cup cherry tomatoes, halved
- 1 tablespoon olive oil
- Salt and pepper to taste
- A sprinkle of red pepper flakes (optional)

- **Instructions**:

1. Toast the whole grain bread to your desired crispness.
2. Mash avocado with a fork and spread it over the toast.
3. Top with cherry tomatoes, a drizzle of olive oil, and season with salt, pepper, and red pepper flakes if desired.

- **Benefits**: Avocado provides healthy fats and fiber, while cherry tomatoes add antioxidants and vitamins.

Recipe 2: Hummus and Cucumber Toast

- **Ingredients**:
  - 1 slice whole grain bread
  - 1/4 cup hummus
  - 1/4 cucumber, thinly sliced
  - 1 tablespoon sesame seeds
  - Fresh dill or parsley for garnish

- **Instructions**:

1. Toast the whole grain bread until golden brown.
2. Spread hummus evenly over the toast.

3. Top with cucumber slices, sesame seeds, and garnish with fresh dill or parsley.
- **Benefits**: Hummus provides protein and fiber, while cucumber adds freshness

Chapter 6: Liver-Friendly Lunch Recipes

A liver-friendly lunch should be packed with nutrients that support liver health and overall well-being. Salads and bowls are excellent choices for lunch as they can be easily customized with a variety of wholesome ingredients. These recipes focus on providing essential vitamins, minerals, and antioxidants while avoiding ingredients that may exacerbate liver issues.

Salads and Bowls

Overview: Salads and bowls are versatile and can include a variety of fresh vegetables, whole grains, lean proteins, and healthy fats. They are rich in nutrients that support liver health, reduce inflammation, and promote detoxification.

Quinoa Salad

Overview: Quinoa is a nutritious whole grain that is high in protein and fiber. It provides essential amino acids and helps maintain stable blood sugar levels, which is beneficial for liver health.

Recipe: Quinoa and Black Bean Salad

- **Ingredients**:
    - 1 cup quinoa, rinsed
    - 2 cups water or low-sodium vegetable broth
    - 1 cup black beans, cooked or canned (rinsed and drained)
    - 1/2 cup corn kernels (fresh or frozen)

- 1 red bell pepper, diced
- 1/4 cup red onion, finely chopped
- 1/4 cup fresh cilantro, chopped
- Juice of 1 lime
- 2 tablespoons extra virgin olive oil
- Salt and pepper to taste
- Optional: 1 avocado, diced

- **Instructions**:

1. In a medium saucepan, combine quinoa and water or vegetable broth. Bring to a boil, then reduce heat to low, cover, and simmer for 15 minutes or until quinoa is cooked and water is absorbed. Let it cool.

2. In a large bowl, combine cooked quinoa, black beans, corn, red bell pepper, red onion, and cilantro.

3. In a small bowl, whisk together lime juice, olive oil, salt, and pepper.

4. Pour the dressing over the quinoa mixture and toss to combine.

5. If desired, gently fold in diced avocado just before serving.

- **Benefits**: Quinoa is a complete protein source and high in fiber. Black beans provide additional protein and fiber, while vegetables and avocado add vitamins, minerals, and healthy fats. Lime juice and cilantro offer antioxidants and flavor without added sugars or unhealthy fats.

Recipe: Quinoa and Roasted Vegetable Salad

- **Ingredients**:
  - 1 cup quinoa, rinsed

- 2 cups water or low-sodium vegetable broth
- 1 cup cherry tomatoes, halved
- 1 cup zucchini, diced
- 1 cup bell peppers (red, yellow, or orange), diced
- 2 tablespoons extra virgin olive oil
- 1 teaspoon dried oregano
- 1/4 cup feta cheese (optional)
- 1/4 cup fresh basil, chopped
- Juice of 1 lemon
- Salt and pepper to taste

- **Instructions**:

1. Preheat the oven to 400°F (200°C). Toss cherry tomatoes, zucchini, and bell peppers with olive oil, oregano, salt, and pepper. Spread them on a baking sheet and roast for 20-25 minutes, or until tender.

2. While the vegetables are roasting, cook quinoa according to package instructions. Let it cool.

3. In a large bowl, combine cooked quinoa, roasted vegetables, and feta cheese if using.

4. Whisk together lemon juice, a bit more olive oil if desired, and season with salt and pepper.

5. Pour the dressing over the salad and toss gently.

6. Garnish with fresh basil before serving.

- **Benefits**: This salad is rich in antioxidants from the roasted vegetables and quinoa provides a complete protein source. The use of olive oil and fresh lemon juice supports liver function and adds healthy fats and vitamin C.

Mediterranean Bowl

Overview: Mediterranean bowls are a great way to incorporate a variety of fresh ingredients and flavors. They are known for their health benefits, including reducing inflammation and supporting cardiovascular and liver health.

Recipe: Mediterranean Chickpea Bowl

- **Ingredients**:
    - 1 cup cooked chickpeas (or 1 can, rinsed and drained)
    - 1 cup cooked brown rice or quinoa
    - 1/2 cup cherry tomatoes, halved
    - 1/2 cucumber, diced
    - 1/4 cup red onion, finely chopped
    - 1/4 cup kalamata olives, sliced
    - 1/4 cup crumbled feta cheese (optional)
    - 2 tablespoons extra virgin olive oil
    - Juice of 1 lemon
    - 1 teaspoon dried oregano
    - Salt and pepper to taste
    - Fresh parsley or mint for garnish
- **Instructions:**

1. In a large bowl, combine cooked chickpeas, brown rice or quinoa, cherry tomatoes, cucumber, red onion, olives, and feta cheese if using.

2. In a small bowl, whisk together olive oil, lemon juice, oregano, salt, and pepper.

3. Pour the dressing over the bowl and toss to combine.

4. Garnish with fresh parsley or mint before serving.

- **Benefits**: Chickpeas are high in protein and fiber, which help stabilize blood sugar levels. The fresh vegetables add vitamins and antioxidants, while olive oil and lemon juice offer healthy fats and vitamin C. Feta cheese adds flavor and a touch of calcium if desired.

Recipe: Greek-Inspired Chicken Bowl

- **Ingredients**:
    - 1 cup cooked farro or brown rice
    - 1 cup grilled chicken breast, sliced
    - 1/2 cup roasted red peppers, sliced
    - 1/2 cup cherry tomatoes, halved
    - 1/4 cup red onion, finely chopped
    - 1/4 cup Kalamata olives, sliced
    - 2 tablespoons tzatziki sauce (store-bought or homemade)
    - 1 tablespoon extra virgin olive oil
    - Fresh dill or parsley for garnish
    - Salt and pepper to taste

- **Instructions**:

1. In a bowl, arrange cooked farro or brown rice as the base.

2. Top with grilled chicken, roasted red peppers, cherry tomatoes, red onion, and olives.

3. Drizzle with olive oil and top with a dollop of tzatziki sauce.

4. Garnish with fresh dill or parsley and season with salt and pepper to taste.

- **Benefits**: This bowl incorporates lean protein from chicken, whole grains, and a variety of vegetables. Tzatziki adds flavor and probiotics, which support digestive health. Olive oil provides healthy fats, which are important for liver function.

Soups and Stews

Soups and stews are excellent choices for liver-friendly lunches as they can be packed with nutrient-dense ingredients that support liver health. These comforting dishes are not only easy to prepare but also versatile and satisfying. They provide a range of essential vitamins, minerals, and antioxidants while helping to maintain hydration and promote detoxification.

Lentil Soup

Overview: Lentils are a fantastic source of plant-based protein and fiber, which are beneficial for liver health. They are low in fat and rich in essential nutrients like iron, folate, and magnesium. Lentil soup is a hearty and nourishing option that can be enjoyed year-round.

Recipe: Hearty Lentil Soup

- **Ingredients**:
    - 1 cup dried green or brown lentils, rinsed and drained
    - 1 tablespoon olive oil
    - 1 onion, chopped
    - 2 cloves garlic, minced
    - 2 carrots, diced
    - 2 celery stalks, diced
    - 1 cup diced tomatoes (canned or fresh)
    - 6 cups low-sodium vegetable broth or water
    - 1 teaspoon ground cumin
    - 1 teaspoon smoked paprika
    - 1/2 teaspoon turmeric
    - 1 bay leaf
    - Salt and pepper to taste
    - 2 cups fresh spinach or kale, chopped
    - 1 tablespoon lemon juice (optional)

- **Instructions**:

1. Heat olive oil in a large pot over medium heat. Add onions and garlic, sautéing until softened.

2. Add carrots and celery, cooking for another 5 minutes until vegetables start to soften.

3. Stir in diced tomatoes, lentils, vegetable broth, cumin, smoked paprika, turmeric, and bay leaf.

4. Bring to a boil, then reduce heat and simmer for 30-35 minutes, or until lentils are tender.

5. Remove bay leaf, stir in fresh spinach or kale, and cook for an additional 5 minutes until greens are wilted.

6. Season with salt, pepper, and lemon juice if desired.

7. Serve hot, and enjoy.

- **Benefits**: Lentils provide a high amount of protein and fiber, supporting liver health by helping to regulate blood sugar levels and improve digestion. The addition of vegetables and spices like turmeric and cumin adds anti-inflammatory properties and enhances the soup's flavor.

Recipe: Spicy Lentil and Sweet Potato Soup

- **Ingredients**:
    - 1 cup dried red or green lentils, rinsed
    - 2 tablespoons olive oil
    - 1 onion, chopped
    - 3 cloves garlic, minced
    - 1 sweet potato, peeled and diced
    - 1 bell pepper, diced
    - 1 can (14.5 oz) diced tomatoes
    - 6 cups low-sodium vegetable broth
    - 1 teaspoon ground coriander

- o 1 teaspoon chili powder
- o 1/2 teaspoon cayenne pepper (optional for heat)
- o Salt and pepper to taste
- o Fresh cilantro or parsley for garnish

- **Instructions**:

1. Heat olive oil in a large pot over medium heat. Add onion and garlic, cooking until translucent.

2. Add sweet potato and bell pepper, cooking for about 5 minutes.

3. Stir in lentils, diced tomatoes, vegetable broth, coriander, chili powder, and cayenne pepper if using.

4. Bring to a boil, then reduce heat and simmer for 25-30 minutes, or until lentils and sweet potatoes are tender.

5. Season with salt and pepper, and garnish with fresh cilantro or parsley before serving.

- **Benefits**: Sweet potatoes are rich in vitamins A and C, while lentils provide protein and fiber. Spices like chili powder and cayenne pepper add a kick of flavor and may boost metabolism.

Vegetable Stew

Overview: Vegetable stews are an excellent way to incorporate a variety of vegetables into your diet. They are low in calories and high in nutrients, making them a great choice for supporting liver function.

Recipe: Classic Vegetable Stew

- **Ingredients**:
    - 2 tablespoons olive oil
    - 1 onion, chopped
    - 2 cloves garlic, minced
    - 2 carrots, sliced
    - 2 celery stalks, sliced
    - 1 cup green beans, chopped
    - 1 cup potatoes, diced
    - 1 cup butternut squash, peeled and diced
    - 1 can (14.5 oz) diced tomatoes
    - 4 cups low-sodium vegetable broth
    - 1 teaspoon dried thyme
    - 1 teaspoon dried rosemary
    - 1/2 teaspoon paprika
    - Salt and pepper to taste
    - 2 cups spinach or kale, chopped

- **Instructions**:

1. Heat olive oil in a large pot over medium heat. Add onion and garlic, sautéing until softened.

2. Add carrots, celery, green beans, potatoes, and butternut squash. Cook for about 5 minutes.

3. Stir in diced tomatoes, vegetable broth, thyme, rosemary, and paprika.

4. Bring to a boil, then reduce heat and simmer for 25-30 minutes, or until vegetables are tender.

5. Add spinach or kale and cook for another 5 minutes.

6. Season with salt and pepper to taste before serving.

- **Benefits**: This vegetable stew is loaded with vitamins and minerals from a variety of vegetables. Olive oil provides healthy fats, while herbs and spices offer additional antioxidants and flavor.

Recipe: Mediterranean Vegetable Stew

- **Ingredients**:
    - 2 tablespoons extra virgin olive oil
    - 1 onion, chopped
    - 3 cloves garlic, minced
    - 1 eggplant, diced
    - 1 zucchini, diced
    - 1 red bell pepper, diced
    - 1 can (14.5 oz) diced tomatoes
    - 1 can (15 oz) chickpeas, rinsed and drained
    - 4 cups low-sodium vegetable broth
    - 1 teaspoon dried oregano
    - 1 teaspoon dried basil
    - 1/2 teaspoon ground cumin

- Salt and pepper to taste
- Fresh basil or parsley for garnish

- **Instructions**:

1. Heat olive oil in a large pot over medium heat. Add onion and garlic, cooking until softened.

2. Add eggplant, zucchini, and red bell pepper, cooking for about 5 minutes.

3. Stir in diced tomatoes, chickpeas, vegetable broth, oregano, basil, and cumin.

4. Bring to a boil, then reduce heat and simmer for 20-25 minutes, or until vegetables are tender.

5. Season with salt and pepper, and garnish with fresh basil or parsley before serving.

- **Benefits**: Eggplant and zucchini provide fiber and antioxidants, while chickpeas add protein. This stew is packed with Mediterranean flavors and supports liver health through its rich vegetable content and healthy fats from olive oil.

Wraps and Sandwiches

Overview: Wraps and sandwiches offer convenience and can be easily packed with fresh, healthy ingredients. By choosing whole grain breads, lean proteins, and a variety of vegetables, you can create satisfying and liver-friendly meals.

Hummus Wrap

Overview: Hummus is a nutrient-rich spread made from chickpeas that provides protein, fiber, and healthy fats. Combined with fresh vegetables and whole grain wraps, it makes for a delicious and liver-friendly lunch.

Recipe: Classic Hummus Wrap

- **Ingredients**:
    - 1 large whole grain tortilla or wrap
    - 1/4 cup hummus (store-bought or homemade)
    - 1/2 cup baby spinach leaves
    - 1/4 cup shredded carrots
    - 1/4 cup sliced cucumbers
    - 1/4 cup cherry tomatoes, halved
    - 1/4 avocado, sliced
    - 1 tablespoon sunflower seeds
    - Salt and pepper to taste
    - Optional: a squeeze of lemon juice or a sprinkle of smoked paprika

- **Instructions**:

1. Lay the whole grain tortilla flat on a clean surface.

2. Spread hummus evenly over the entire surface of the tortilla.

3. Arrange spinach leaves, shredded carrots, cucumbers, cherry tomatoes, and avocado slices in a line down the center of the tortilla.

4. Sprinkle sunflower seeds over the vegetables.

5. Season with salt, pepper, and optional lemon juice or smoked paprika.

6. Roll up the tortilla tightly, folding in the sides as you go.

7. Cut in half and serve immediately or wrap in parchment paper for an on-the-go meal.

- **Benefits**: Hummus provides protein and fiber, supporting liver health. Vegetables and avocado add vitamins, minerals, and healthy fats. Whole grain tortillas offer additional fiber, aiding in digestion.

Recipe: Spicy Hummus and Veggie Wrap

- **Ingredients**:
    - 1 large whole grain tortilla
    - 1/4 cup spicy hummus (or regular hummus mixed with a dash of hot sauce)
    - 1/2 cup mixed greens (e.g., arugula, kale, or lettuce)
    - 1/4 cup red bell peppers, thinly sliced
    - 1/4 cup shredded red cabbage
    - 1/4 cup cooked quinoa (optional)
    - 1 tablespoon pumpkin seeds
    - A squeeze of lime juice
    - Salt and pepper to taste
- **Instructions**:

1. Spread the spicy hummus evenly over the tortilla.

2. Layer mixed greens, red bell peppers, shredded cabbage, and quinoa if using.

3. Sprinkle with pumpkin seeds and a squeeze of lime juice.
4. Season with salt and pepper.
5. Roll up the tortilla tightly, folding in the sides as you roll.
6. Slice in half and serve.

- **Benefits**: Spicy hummus adds a kick while still providing protein and fiber. The variety of vegetables offers antioxidants and vitamins, while quinoa and pumpkin seeds add extra protein and healthy fats.

Grilled Veggie Sandwich

Overview: A grilled veggie sandwich can be a satisfying and flavorful meal. By using whole grain bread and incorporating a variety of colorful vegetables, you create a dish that supports liver health.

Recipe: Mediterranean Grilled Veggie Sandwich

- **Ingredients**:
    - 2 slices whole grain bread
    - 1/4 cup hummus
    - 1/2 cup grilled zucchini slices
    - 1/4 cup roasted red peppers, sliced
    - 1/4 cup eggplant slices, grilled
    - 1/4 cup kalamata olives, sliced
    - 1/4 cup crumbled feta cheese (optional)
    - 1 tablespoon extra virgin olive oil

- Fresh basil or oregano for garnish
- Salt and pepper to taste

- **Instructions**:

1. Spread hummus on one side of each slice of whole grain bread.

2. Layer grilled zucchini, roasted red peppers, grilled eggplant, and olives on one slice of bread.

3. If desired, sprinkle with crumbled feta cheese.

4. Top with the second slice of bread, hummus side down.

5. Heat a grill pan over medium heat and brush with olive oil.

6. Grill the sandwich for 2-3 minutes on each side, or until the bread is golden and the vegetables are heated through.

7. Garnish with fresh basil or oregano and season with salt and pepper.

- **Benefits**: Whole grain bread provides fiber, while grilled vegetables offer antioxidants and essential nutrients. Hummus and feta cheese add protein and healthy fats, supporting liver health.

Recipe: Turkey and Avocado Sandwich

- **Ingredients**:
  - 2 slices whole grain bread
  - 3-4 slices of lean turkey breast
  - 1/4 avocado, mashed
  - 1/4 cup spinach leaves
  - 1/4 cup sliced tomatoes

- o 1/4 cup shredded lettuce
- o 1 tablespoon Dijon mustard
- o Salt and pepper to taste
- **Instructions**:

1. Spread mashed avocado on one side of each slice of bread.

2. On one slice of bread, layer turkey slices, spinach leaves, tomatoes, and shredded lettuce.

3. Spread Dijon mustard on the other slice of bread.

4. Close the sandwich, slice in half if desired, and serve.

- **Benefits**: Lean turkey provides high-quality protein, while avocado offers healthy fats and fiber. Whole grain bread adds additional fiber, and vegetables contribute essential vitamins and minerals.

Liver-friendly wraps and sandwiches can be both nutritious and satisfying. By focusing on ingredients such as whole grains, lean proteins, fresh vegetables, and healthy fats, you create balanced meals that support liver health. Hummus, grilled vegetables, and lean turkey are excellent choices for these meals, providing essential nutrients while avoiding excess sugars and unhealthy fats. These recipes are designed to be easy to prepare and adaptable to your taste preferences, making it easier to enjoy healthy lunches while caring for your liver.

Chapter 7: Liver-Friendly Dinner Recipes

Dinner is a crucial meal for maintaining overall health and supporting liver function. Liver-friendly dinner recipes should focus on lean proteins, whole grains, and plenty of vegetables. Here's an extensive guide to liver-friendly main courses that are not only delicious but also supportive of liver health.

Main Courses

Overview: Liver-friendly main courses can provide essential nutrients while minimizing ingredients that might strain liver function. Lean proteins like fish and chicken, combined with a variety of vegetables and legumes, create balanced and healthful meals.

Baked Fish with Herbs

Overview: Baking fish with herbs is a simple and effective way to prepare a liver-friendly dinner. Fish is a high-quality protein that supports liver health and provides essential omega-3 fatty acids.

Recipe: Herb-Crusted Baked Salmon

- **Ingredients**:
    - 4 salmon fillets (about 6 oz each)
    - 2 tablespoons extra virgin olive oil
    - 2 tablespoons fresh parsley, chopped
    - 1 tablespoon fresh dill, chopped
    - 1 tablespoon fresh thyme, chopped
    - 2 cloves garlic, minced
    - Juice of 1 lemon
    - Salt and pepper to taste
    - Lemon wedges for serving
- **Instructions**:

1. Preheat your oven to 375°F (190°C).

2. Place the salmon fillets on a baking sheet lined with parchment paper.

3. In a small bowl, mix olive oil, parsley, dill, thyme, garlic, lemon juice, salt, and pepper.

4. Rub the herb mixture evenly over the salmon fillets.

5. Bake for 15-20 minutes, or until the salmon is cooked through and flakes easily with a fork.

6. Serve with lemon wedges on the side.

- **Benefits**: Salmon is rich in omega-3 fatty acids and protein, which are beneficial for liver health. Fresh herbs add flavor without excess salt, and lemon juice provides a boost of vitamin C, enhancing the overall nutritional profile.

Recipe: Baked Cod with Lemon and Capers

- **Ingredients**:
    - 4 cod fillets (about 6 oz each)
    - 1 tablespoon extra virgin olive oil
    - Juice of 1 lemon
    - 2 tablespoons capers, rinsed and drained
    - 2 cloves garlic, minced
    - 1 teaspoon dried oregano
    - Salt and pepper to taste
- **Instructions**:

1. Preheat your oven to 400°F (200°C).
2. Place cod fillets on a baking dish.
3. Drizzle with olive oil and lemon juice.
4. Sprinkle capers, garlic, oregano, salt, and pepper over the fillets.
5. Bake for 12-15 minutes, or until the fish is opaque and flakes easily.

- **Benefits**: Cod is a low-fat, high-protein fish that is gentle on the liver. Capers and lemon add flavor and antioxidants without extra calories or unhealthy fats.

Chicken and Vegetable Stir-Fry

Overview: Stir-frying is a quick and healthy cooking method that retains the nutrients in vegetables while using minimal oil. Chicken provides lean protein, and a variety of vegetables ensure a range of vitamins and minerals.

Recipe: Ginger-Sesame Chicken Stir-Fry

- **Ingredients**:
    - 1 lb (450g) chicken breast, thinly sliced
    - 2 tablespoons extra virgin olive oil
    - 2 cups broccoli florets
    - 1 cup bell peppers, sliced (red, yellow, or green)
    - 1 cup snap peas
    - 1 tablespoon fresh ginger, grated
    - 2 cloves garlic, minced
    - 2 tablespoons low-sodium soy sauce
    - 1 tablespoon sesame seeds
    - 1 tablespoon rice vinegar
    - Salt and pepper to taste

- **Instructions**:

1. Heat olive oil in a large skillet or wok over medium-high heat.
2. Add chicken and cook until browned and cooked through, about 5-7 minutes.
3. Remove chicken from the skillet and set aside.

4. In the same skillet, add broccoli, bell peppers, and snap peas. Stir-fry for 3-4 minutes until vegetables are tender-crisp.

5. Add ginger, garlic, soy sauce, and rice vinegar. Stir well to combine.

6. Return the chicken to the skillet and toss to coat in the sauce and heat through.

7. Sprinkle with sesame seeds before serving.

- **Benefits**: Chicken provides lean protein, while a variety of vegetables contribute essential vitamins, minerals, and fiber. Ginger and garlic offer anti-inflammatory benefits, and sesame seeds add healthy fats.

Recipe: Teriyaki Chicken and Vegetable Stir-Fry

- **Ingredients**:
    - 1 lb (450g) chicken thighs, boneless and skinless, cut into strips
    - 2 tablespoons extra virgin olive oil
    - 2 cups bell peppers, sliced
    - 1 cup carrots, thinly sliced
    - 1 cup broccoli florets
    - 1/4 cup low-sodium teriyaki sauce
    - 1 tablespoon fresh ginger, grated
    - 2 cloves garlic, minced
    - 1 tablespoon sesame seeds
    - Cooked brown rice or quinoa for serving

- **Instructions**:

1. Heat olive oil in a large pan or wok over medium heat.

2. Add chicken strips and cook until browned and cooked through, about 6-8 minutes.

3. Remove chicken and set aside.

4. Add bell peppers, carrots, and broccoli to the pan. Stir-fry for 4-5 minutes until vegetables are tender.

5. Return the chicken to the pan and add teriyaki sauce, ginger, and garlic. Stir well to coat everything in the sauce and heat through.

6. Sprinkle with sesame seeds and serve over brown rice or quinoa.

- **Benefits**: Chicken thighs provide a bit more flavor while still being a good source of protein. Teriyaki sauce adds a touch of sweetness without added sugars. Vegetables offer a range of nutrients and fiber.

Lentil and Vegetable Curry

Overview: Lentils are an excellent source of plant-based protein and fiber. Combined with a variety of vegetables and spices, lentil curry is a flavorful and filling meal that supports liver health.

Recipe: Spicy Lentil and Vegetable Curry

- **Ingredients**:
    - 1 cup dried green or brown lentils, rinsed
    - 2 tablespoons extra virgin olive oil
    - 1 large onion, chopped
    - 2 cloves garlic, minced

- 1 tablespoon fresh ginger, grated
- 1 cup carrots, diced
- 1 cup cauliflower florets
- 1 cup spinach leaves
- 1 can (14.5 oz) diced tomatoes
- 1 can (14.5 oz) coconut milk
- 2 tablespoons curry powder
- 1 teaspoon turmeric
- 1 teaspoon cumin
- Salt and pepper to taste
- Fresh cilantro for garnish

- **Instructions**:

1. In a large pot, heat olive oil over medium heat.

2. Add onion, garlic, and ginger. Cook until the onion is translucent, about 5 minutes.

3. Stir in curry powder, turmeric, and cumin, and cook for an additional 1-2 minutes.

4. Add carrots, cauliflower, lentils, diced tomatoes, and coconut milk.

5. Bring to a boil, then reduce heat and simmer for 30-35 minutes, or until lentils and vegetables are tender.

6. Stir in spinach leaves and cook for an additional 5 minutes.

7. Season with salt and pepper. Garnish with fresh cilantro before serving.

- **Benefits**: Lentils provide protein and fiber, supporting liver health and digestion. Vegetables and coconut milk add essential nutrients and healthy fats. Spices like turmeric and cumin have anti-inflammatory properties.

Recipe: Creamy Lentil and Vegetable Stew

- **Ingredients**:
    - 1 cup dried red lentils, rinsed
    - 1 tablespoon extra virgin olive oil
    - 1 large onion, chopped
    - 2 cloves garlic, minced
    - 1 cup sweet potatoes, peeled and diced
    - 1 cup green beans, trimmed and cut
    - 1 can (14.5 oz) diced tomatoes
    - 1 can (14.5 oz) light coconut milk
    - 1 teaspoon smoked paprika
    - 1/2 teaspoon ground coriander
    - 1/2 teaspoon ground cumin
    - Salt and pepper to taste
    - Fresh parsley for garnish

- **Instructions**:

1. In a large pot, heat olive oil over medium heat.

2. Add onion and garlic, cooking until the onion is translucent, about 5 minutes.

3. Stir in paprika, coriander, and cumin. Cook for 1-2 minutes.

4. Add sweet potatoes, green beans, lentils, diced tomatoes, and coconut milk.

5. Bring to a boil, then reduce heat and simmer for 25-30 minutes, or until lentils and vegetables are tender.

6. Season with salt and pepper. Garnish with fresh parsley before serving.

- **Benefits**: Red lentils are quick-cooking and rich in protein and fiber. Sweet potatoes and green beans provide vitamins and minerals, while coconut milk adds a creamy texture without excess calories.

Liver-friendly dinner recipes should include lean proteins, whole grains, and plenty of vegetables. Baked fish with herbs, chicken and vegetable stir-fry, and lentil and vegetable curry are excellent choices for a nutritious and balanced dinner. These recipes focus on supporting liver health by incorporating nutrient-dense ingredients while avoiding excessive sugars and unhealthy fats. Each recipe is designed to be flavorful and satisfying, ensuring you enjoy your meals while promoting overall well-being.

Side dishes

When planning a liver-friendly dinner, side dishes play a vital role in complementing the main course and ensuring a well-rounded, nutritious meal. Opting for simple, nutrient-dense sides like steamed vegetables and quinoa pilaf can enhance liver health while adding variety and flavor to your meals. Here's an extensive guide to preparing liver-friendly side dishes.

Steamed Vegetables

Overview: Steaming vegetables is one of the best methods for preserving their nutrients while keeping the preparation simple. Vegetables are rich in vitamins, minerals, and antioxidants that support liver function and overall health.

Recipe: Classic Steamed Vegetable Medley

- **Ingredients**:
    - 1 cup broccoli florets
    - 1 cup carrots, sliced
    - 1 cup cauliflower florets
    - 1 cup snap peas
    - 1 tablespoon extra virgin olive oil
    - 1 teaspoon lemon zest
    - Salt and pepper to taste
    - Optional: a pinch of dried herbs such as thyme or rosemary
- **Instructions**:

1. Prepare a steamer basket over a pot of simmering water.

2. Place the broccoli, carrots, cauliflower, and snap peas in the steamer basket.

3. Cover and steam for 5-7 minutes, or until the vegetables are tender but still crisp.

4. Transfer vegetables to a serving bowl.

5. Drizzle with olive oil, and sprinkle with lemon zest, salt, and pepper.

6. Add a pinch of dried herbs if desired for extra flavor.
7. Serve immediately.

- **Benefits**: Steamed vegetables retain their vitamins and minerals, making them a highly nutritious addition to any meal. Olive oil adds healthy fats, while lemon zest provides a refreshing flavor without extra calories.

Recipe: Ginger-Sesame Steamed Vegetables

- **Ingredients**:
    - 1 cup baby bok choy, halved
    - 1 cup shiitake mushrooms, sliced
    - 1 cup bell peppers, sliced
    - 1 tablespoon fresh ginger, grated
    - 1 tablespoon low-sodium soy sauce
    - 1 teaspoon sesame oil
    - 1 teaspoon sesame seeds
    - Salt and pepper to taste
- **Instructions**:

1. Set up a steamer basket over a pot of simmering water.
2. Place bok choy, mushrooms, and bell peppers in the steamer basket.
3. Cover and steam for 4-6 minutes, until vegetables are tender.
4. In a small bowl, mix ginger, soy sauce, and sesame oil.
5. Drizzle the ginger-soy mixture over the steamed vegetables.

6. Sprinkle with sesame seeds and season with salt and pepper.
7. Serve warm.

- **Benefits**: Bok choy and shiitake mushrooms provide a range of nutrients, including antioxidants and vitamins. Ginger and sesame oil add flavor and additional health benefits, such as anti-inflammatory properties.

Quinoa Pilaf

Overview: Quinoa is a highly nutritious grain that is a complete protein, containing all nine essential amino acids. Quinoa pilaf is a versatile side dish that pairs well with many main courses and adds a nutritious boost to your meal.

Recipe: Herb-Infused Quinoa Pilaf

- **Ingredients**:
    - 1 cup quinoa, rinsed
    - 2 cups low-sodium vegetable broth
    - 1 tablespoon extra virgin olive oil
    - 1 small onion, finely chopped
    - 2 cloves garlic, minced
    - 1/2 cup diced bell peppers (any color)
    - 1/2 cup chopped fresh parsley
    - 1/4 cup chopped fresh basil
    - 1/4 cup sliced almonds
    - Salt and pepper to taste

- **Instructions**:

1. In a medium saucepan, heat olive oil over medium heat.

2. Add onion and garlic, cooking until the onion is translucent, about 5 minutes.

3. Stir in diced bell peppers and cook for an additional 2 minutes.

4. Add quinoa and vegetable broth. Bring to a boil.

5. Reduce heat to low, cover, and simmer for 15 minutes, or until quinoa is cooked and liquid is absorbed.

6. Fluff quinoa with a fork and stir in parsley, basil, and sliced almonds.

7. Season with salt and pepper before serving.

- **Benefits**: Quinoa is a complete protein and rich in fiber, aiding in digestion and liver health. Fresh herbs like parsley and basil provide antioxidants, while almonds add healthy fats and a crunchy texture.

Recipe: Lemon and Dill Quinoa Pilaf

- **Ingredients**:
    - 1 cup quinoa, rinsed
    - 2 cups water
    - 1 tablespoon extra virgin olive oil
    - 1 small onion, diced
    - 1/2 cup frozen peas, thawed
    - 1 tablespoon lemon juice

- o   2 tablespoons fresh dill, chopped
- o   Salt and pepper to taste

- **Instructions**:

1. In a medium saucepan, heat olive oil over medium heat.
2. Add onion and cook until translucent, about 5 minutes.
3. Stir in quinoa and cook for 1-2 minutes.
4. Add water and bring to a boil.
5. Reduce heat to low, cover, and simmer for 15 minutes, or until quinoa is tender and water is absorbed.
6. Stir in peas, lemon juice, and fresh dill.
7. Season with salt and pepper before serving.

- **Benefits**: This quinoa pilaf provides a zesty flavor with lemon juice and dill. Peas add additional vitamins and minerals, and the use of olive oil ensures healthy fats.

Liver-friendly side dishes can enhance your main courses while contributing essential nutrients to support liver health. Steamed vegetables are a simple and effective way to enjoy a variety of nutrients while retaining the natural flavors of the vegetables. Quinoa pilaf offers a nutrient-dense, protein-rich alternative to traditional grains. By focusing on fresh ingredients and minimizing added fats and sugars, these side dishes complement a liver-friendly diet and contribute to overall well-being.

Healthy Desserts

Overview: Liver-friendly desserts should focus on natural sweetness from fruits and minimal added sugars. They should also include ingredients that provide additional nutrients to support liver health.

Fruit Salad

Overview: Fruit salad is a versatile and refreshing dessert that can be tailored to include a variety of fruits. It's an excellent source of vitamins, minerals, and antioxidants, which are beneficial for liver health.

Recipe: Citrus and Berry Fruit Salad

- **Ingredients**:
    - 1 cup strawberries, hulled and sliced
    - 1 cup blueberries
    - 1 cup kiwi, peeled and diced
    - 1 orange, peeled and segmented
    - 1/2 grapefruit, peeled and segmented
    - 1 tablespoon honey or agave syrup (optional, for added sweetness)
    - 1 tablespoon fresh mint leaves, chopped

- **Instructions**:

1. In a large bowl, combine strawberries, blueberries, kiwi, orange, and grapefruit.

2. If desired, drizzle honey or agave syrup over the fruit for added sweetness.

3. Gently toss to mix.

4. Sprinkle with fresh mint leaves before serving.

5. Serve immediately or chill in the refrigerator for about 30 minutes.

- **Benefits**: This fruit salad provides a range of antioxidants from berries and citrus fruits, which support liver health. Kiwi is high in vitamin C, while grapefruit contains compounds that can aid liver detoxification. Mint adds a refreshing flavor without extra calories.

Recipe: Tropical Fruit Salad with Lime Dressing

- **Ingredients**:
    - 1 cup pineapple chunks
    - 1 cup mango chunks
    - 1 cup papaya chunks
    - 1/2 cup shredded coconut (unsweetened)
    - Juice of 1 lime
    - 1 tablespoon fresh cilantro, chopped
- **Instructions**:

1. In a large bowl, combine pineapple, mango, papaya, and shredded coconut.
2. Drizzle lime juice over the fruit and toss gently.
3. Sprinkle with fresh cilantro before serving.
4. Serve immediately or chill in the refrigerator for about 30 minutes.

- **Benefits**: Pineapple, mango, and papaya are rich in vitamins and enzymes that support digestion and liver health. Lime juice adds a tangy flavor while providing vitamin C, and cilantro contributes additional antioxidants.

Baked Apples

Overview: Baked apples are a warm and comforting dessert that can be naturally sweetened with spices and a small amount of honey or maple syrup. Apples are high in fiber and antioxidants, making them a great choice for liver health.

Recipe: Cinnamon and Walnut Baked Apples

- **Ingredients**:
    - 4 medium apples (such as Granny Smith or Fuji)
    - 1/4 cup walnuts, chopped
    - 2 tablespoons raisins or dried cranberries
    - 1 tablespoon honey or maple syrup
    - 1 teaspoon ground cinnamon
    - 1/2 teaspoon ground nutmeg
    - Optional: a small pat of unsalted butter for extra richness

- **Instructions**:

1. Preheat your oven to 350°F (175°C).
2. Core the apples, creating a hollow center without piercing the bottom.
3. In a small bowl, mix chopped walnuts, raisins or cranberries, honey or maple syrup, cinnamon, and nutmeg.
4. Stuff the apple cores with the walnut mixture.
5. Place the apples in a baking dish. If desired, place a small pat of butter on top of each apple.
6. Bake for 25-30 minutes, or until the apples are tender.

7. Serve warm.

- **Benefits**: Apples are a good source of fiber and antioxidants. Walnuts provide healthy fats and additional fiber, while cinnamon and nutmeg add flavor without extra calories. The optional butter can add richness but is not necessary for a liver-friendly option.

Recipe: Apple and Pear Crisp

- **Ingredients**:
    - 2 apples, peeled, cored, and sliced
    - 2 pears, peeled, cored, and sliced
    - 1 tablespoon lemon juice
    - 1/4 cup rolled oats
    - 1/4 cup almond flour
    - 2 tablespoons almond butter
    - 1 tablespoon honey or maple syrup
    - 1 teaspoon ground cinnamon
    - 1/2 teaspoon ground ginger
- **Instructions**:

1. Preheat your oven to 375°F (190°C).
2. In a bowl, toss apples and pears with lemon juice.
3. Transfer the fruit to a baking dish.
4. In a separate bowl, combine oats, almond flour, almond butter, honey or maple syrup, cinnamon, and ginger. Mix until crumbly.
5. Sprinkle the oat mixture over the fruit.

6.   Bake for 25-30 minutes, or until the topping is golden and the fruit is tender.

7.   Serve warm or at room temperature.

- **Benefits**: Apples and pears provide fiber and essential nutrients, while oats and almond flour offer additional fiber and healthy fats. The use of almond butter and minimal honey keeps the dessert nutritious and satisfying.

Healthy desserts can be both delicious and supportive of liver health when they focus on natural sweetness and nutrient-rich ingredients. Fruit salads offer a refreshing and vitamin-packed option, while baked apples provide a warm, comforting treat. By choosing fruits, nuts, and minimal added sugars, these desserts can enhance your meal while promoting overall liver health.

Chapter 8: Liver-Friendly Drinks and Beverages Recipes

Maintaining a liver-friendly diet involves not only choosing the right foods but also selecting beverages that support liver health. Drinks that are rich in antioxidants, vitamins, and minerals can aid in liver detoxification, reduce inflammation, and promote overall well-being. Below are several liver-friendly drinks and beverages, each with a detailed recipe and description of their health benefits.

1. Green Detox Juice

Ingredients:

- 1 cucumber, peeled and chopped
- 2 celery stalks, chopped
- 1 green apple, cored and chopped
- 1 cup spinach leaves
- 1 lemon, juiced
- 1-inch piece of fresh ginger, peeled
- 1 cup water or coconut water

Instructions:

1. Place all the ingredients in a blender.
2. Blend until smooth.
3. Strain through a fine mesh sieve or cheesecloth if desired for a smoother texture.
4. Serve immediately over ice or chill in the refrigerator.

Benefits:

- **Cucumber** and **celery** are high in water content and help with hydration and flushing out toxins.
- **Green apple** adds a touch of natural sweetness and provides antioxidants.
- **Spinach** is rich in vitamins A and C, which support liver health and detoxification.
- **Lemon** and **ginger** have anti-inflammatory and detoxifying properties.

2. Beetroot and Carrot Juice

Ingredients:

- 1 medium beetroot, peeled and chopped
- 2 carrots, peeled and chopped
- 1 apple, cored and chopped
- 1-inch piece of fresh turmeric, peeled (or 1/2 teaspoon turmeric powder)
- 1 cup water

Instructions:

1. Combine all ingredients in a blender.
2. Blend until smooth.
3. Strain if desired.
4. Serve chilled.

Benefits:

- **Beetroot** contains betaine, which helps in liver detoxification and supports bile production.
- **Carrots** are rich in beta-carotene, which supports liver function and overall health.
- **Turmeric** has powerful anti-inflammatory properties and supports liver function.

3. Lemon Ginger Tea

Ingredients:

- 1 lemon, sliced
- 1-inch piece of fresh ginger, sliced
- 2 cups hot water
- 1 teaspoon honey (optional)

Instructions:

1. Add lemon slices and ginger to a teapot or mug.
2. Pour hot water over the ingredients.
3. Let steep for 5-10 minutes.
4. Strain and add honey if desired.
5. Serve hot.

Benefits:

- **Lemon** provides vitamin C, which helps in liver detoxification.
- **Ginger** aids in digestion and reduces inflammation.
- This tea helps in digestion and detoxification.

4. Mint and Cucumber Infused Water

Ingredients:

- 1 cucumber, sliced
- A handful of fresh mint leaves
- 1 lemon, sliced
- 4 cups water

Instructions:

1. Combine cucumber slices, mint leaves, and lemon slices in a pitcher.
2. Fill with water.
3. Let infuse in the refrigerator for at least 2 hours before serving.

Benefits:

- **Cucumber** helps with hydration and detoxification.
- **Mint** aids in digestion and adds a refreshing flavor.
- **Lemon** provides vitamin C and supports liver function.

5. Berry Antioxidant Smoothie

Ingredients:

- 1/2 cup blueberries
- 1/2 cup strawberries, hulled
- 1/2 cup raspberries
- 1 cup unsweetened almond milk
- 1 tablespoon chia seeds
- 1 tablespoon honey (optional)

Instructions:

1. Place all ingredients in a blender.
2. Blend until smooth.
3. Serve immediately.

Benefits:

- **Berries** are rich in antioxidants, which help protect the liver from damage.
- **Chia seeds** provide omega-3 fatty acids and fiber, supporting overall health.
- **Almond milk** is a non-dairy alternative that's gentle on the liver.

6. Aloe Vera Juice

Ingredients:

- 1/4 cup fresh aloe vera gel
- 1 cup water
- 1 tablespoon lemon juice
- 1 teaspoon honey (optional)

Instructions:

1. Blend aloe vera gel and water until smooth.
2. Add lemon juice and honey, and blend again.
3. Serve chilled.

Benefits:

- **Aloe vera** has anti-inflammatory properties and supports liver health.
- **Lemon juice** aids in detoxification.

7. Celery and Pineapple Juice

Ingredients:

- 2 celery stalks, chopped
- 1 cup pineapple chunks
- 1/2 lemon, juiced
- 1 cup water

Instructions:

1. Blend celery, pineapple, and water until smooth.
2. Strain if desired.
3. Add lemon juice and stir.
4. Serve chilled.

Benefits:

- **Celery** helps with hydration and detoxification.
- **Pineapple** contains bromelain, which aids digestion.
- **Lemon** adds vitamin C and supports liver health.

Liver-friendly drinks and beverages play a crucial role in supporting liver health and overall well-being. These recipes provide a range of options, from hydrating infused waters to nutrient-dense smoothies and juices. They are designed to be rich in antioxidants, vitamins, and minerals that aid in detoxification, reduce inflammation, and support liver function. Incorporate these drinks into your daily routine to complement a liver-healthy diet and lifestyle. Adjust ingredients and sweetness according to your personal preferences and nutritional needs.

Chapter 9: 30 Day Liver-Friendly Meal Plan

Introduction to The 30-Day Meal Plan for a Liver-Friendly Diet

Creating a structured 30-day meal plan can be an effective strategy for improving liver health and overall well-being. This introduction provides a comprehensive guide to setting goals, shopping for the right ingredients, preparing meals efficiently, and implementing weekly meal plans. By following these guidelines, you can establish a sustainable and healthful eating routine that supports liver function and enhances your quality of life.

Goals and Expectations

Overview: The primary goal of a 30-day meal plan for a liver-friendly diet is to support liver health through balanced and nutritious meals. Setting clear, achievable goals and understanding what to expect from the meal plan will help ensure success and make the process more manageable.

Goals:

1. **Improve Liver Health**: Focus on including foods that support liver function, such as fruits, vegetables, lean proteins, and whole grains. Avoid foods high in saturated fats, added sugars, and processed ingredients.

2. **Enhance Nutrient Intake**: Ensure a variety of foods to meet your nutritional needs. This includes adequate vitamins, minerals, and antioxidants that aid in liver detoxification and overall health.

3. **Promote Sustainable Eating Habits**: Develop habits that are easy to maintain long-term, such as cooking at home more often, using fresh ingredients, and understanding portion sizes.

4. **Achieve Balanced Meals**: Each meal should be balanced with appropriate portions of proteins, carbohydrates, and fats to maintain energy levels and support metabolic health.

Expectations:

- **Adaptation Period**: Initially, there might be an adjustment period as you transition to new eating habits. Be patient with yourself and give your body time to adapt.

- **Varied Meals**: The meal plan will include a variety of recipes to keep meals interesting and prevent monotony. Expect to try new foods and flavors.

- **Flexibility**: While the meal plan provides structure, it is flexible. Adjust portions and ingredients based on personal preferences and nutritional needs.

- **Progress Tracking**: Monitor how your body responds to the new eating patterns. Look for improvements in energy levels, digestion, and overall well-being.

Grocery Shopping Tips

Overview: Proper grocery shopping is key to sticking with a liver-friendly meal plan. Knowing what to buy and how to shop efficiently can make meal preparation easier and more enjoyable.

Tips:

1. **Plan Your List**: Start with a detailed grocery list based on the weekly meal plans. This helps avoid impulse buys and ensures you have all the necessary ingredients.

2. **Focus on Fresh Produce**: Prioritize fresh fruits and vegetables. Choose a variety of colors to maximize nutrient intake. Seasonal produce often tastes better and can be more affordable.

3. **Opt for Whole Grains**: Select whole grains such as quinoa, brown rice, and oats. These provide more nutrients and fiber compared to refined grains.

4. **Lean Proteins**: Choose lean proteins like chicken breast, fish, and legumes. Avoid processed meats that can be high in unhealthy fats and sodium.

5. **Healthy Fats**: Include sources of healthy fats such as avocados, nuts, seeds, and olive oil. These fats support liver function and overall health.

6. **Read Labels**: Check ingredient lists for added sugars, sodium, and unhealthy fats. Opt for products with minimal processing and simple, natural ingredients.

7. **Stock Up on Basics**: Keep a stock of pantry staples such as canned beans, low-sodium vegetable broth, and spices. This makes meal preparation quicker and easier.

8. **Buy in Bulk**: Consider buying non-perishable items in bulk, such as grains and legumes. This can be cost-effective and ensures you have key ingredients on hand.

Meal Prep and Planning

Overview: Effective meal prep and planning are essential for sticking to a 30-day meal plan. Preparing meals in advance can save time and reduce stress during busy days.

Meal Prep Tips:

1. **Batch Cooking**: Cook large quantities of staples like grains, beans, and proteins at the beginning of the week. Store them in the refrigerator or freezer for easy use in various meals.

2. **Pre-Chop Vegetables**: Wash, peel, and chop vegetables in advance. Store them in airtight containers in the refrigerator to make meal assembly quicker.

3. **Use Portion Containers**: Invest in portion-controlled containers for easy meal storage and transportation. This helps with portion control and reduces food waste.

4. **Prepare Sauces and Dressings**: Make dressings, marinades, and sauces ahead of time. Store them in the refrigerator to add flavor to your meals quickly.

5. **Label and Date**: Clearly label and date all prepped items. This helps in keeping track of freshness and ensures you use older items first.
6. **Plan Your Week**: Use a weekly planner or digital app to map out meals for each day. This helps with organization and makes grocery shopping more efficient.

Weekly meal plans

Weekly meal plans provide structure and variety, helping to ensure a balanced diet and making meal preparation more manageable. Here's how to create and implement effective weekly meal plans:

How to Create a Weekly Meal Plan:

1. **Review Recipes**: Choose recipes that align with the liver-friendly diet and fit within your time constraints and cooking skills.
2. **Balance Meals**: Ensure each day includes a variety of meals, such as breakfasts, lunches, dinners, and snacks. Incorporate a range of proteins, vegetables, and whole grains.
3. **Include Leftovers**: Plan for leftovers to reduce cooking time and food waste. This can be especially useful for lunches and dinners.
4. **Be Flexible**: Allow for some flexibility in your meal plan to accommodate changes in schedule or unexpected cravings. Swap similar meals if needed.

Benefits:

- **Consistency**: A weekly plan helps maintain consistent eating habits and prevents last-minute unhealthy choices.
- **Time Management**: Reduces daily decision-making and saves time during busy weeks.

- **Variety**: Ensures a variety of nutrients and flavors, preventing dietary boredom.

The 30-day meal plan for a liver-friendly diet aims to support liver health through well-balanced, nutritious meals. Setting clear goals and understanding expectations helps in adhering to the plan. Effective grocery shopping and meal prep are essential for making the process smoother and more enjoyable. Implementing weekly meal plans ensures structure and variety, making it easier to maintain a healthy diet. By following these guidelines, you can successfully integrate liver-friendly eating habits into your lifestyle.

Week 1: Detox and Reset

This first week of the 30-day meal plan is designed to kickstart your journey with a focus on detoxifying and resetting your system. The meals emphasize fresh, nutrient-rich ingredients that support liver health and provide a clean slate for the rest of your diet. Each day features balanced, liver-friendly options for breakfast, lunch, and dinner.

Day 1

- **Breakfast: Smoothie Bowl with Spinach, Banana, and Mixed Berries**
    - Blend 1 cup spinach, 1 banana, 1/2 cup mixed berries, and 1/2 cup unsweetened almond milk. Top with a handful of granola, chia seeds, and fresh berries.

- **Lunch: Quinoa Salad with Chickpeas, Cucumbers, and Cherry Tomatoes**
    - Toss 1 cup cooked quinoa with 1/2 cup chickpeas, 1 cup diced cucumbers, and 1/2 cup halved cherry tomatoes. Dress with lemon juice, olive oil, salt, and pepper.
- **Dinner: Baked Salmon with Steamed Broccoli and Brown Rice**
    - Bake a salmon fillet with lemon slices, garlic, and herbs at 375°F (190°C) for 20 minutes. Serve with 1 cup steamed broccoli and 1/2 cup cooked brown rice.

Day 2

- **Breakfast: Oatmeal with Chia Seeds, Apple Slices, and Cinnamon**
    - Cook 1/2 cup oats with 1 cup water or unsweetened almond milk. Stir in 1 tablespoon chia seeds, top with apple slices, and sprinkle with cinnamon.
- **Lunch: Mediterranean Bowl with Hummus, Roasted Vegetables, and Quinoa**
    - Combine 1/2 cup cooked quinoa with 1/2 cup hummus, 1 cup roasted vegetables (e.g., bell peppers, zucchini, and eggplant), and a sprinkle of feta cheese (optional).
- **Dinner: Chicken and Vegetable Stir-Fry with Brown Rice**
    - Stir-fry 4 oz chicken breast with 2 cups mixed vegetables (e.g., bell peppers, broccoli, and snap peas) in 1 tablespoon olive oil. Serve with 1/2 cup cooked brown rice.

Day 3

- **Breakfast: Liver-Friendly Pancakes with Fresh Strawberries**
    - Make pancakes using 1 cup oat flour, 1/2 cup unsweetened almond milk, and 1 tablespoon flaxseed meal. Top with fresh strawberries and a drizzle of honey (optional).

- **Lunch: Lentil Soup with a Side of Mixed Greens**
    - Prepare lentil soup with 1 cup cooked lentils, diced tomatoes, carrots, celery, and spices. Serve with a side salad of mixed greens dressed with lemon juice and olive oil.

- **Dinner: Grilled Cod with Steamed Carrots and Quinoa**
    - Grill a cod fillet with lemon, garlic, and herbs. Serve with 1 cup steamed carrots and 1/2 cup cooked quinoa.

Day 4

- **Breakfast: Egg and Veggie Scramble with Whole Grain Toast**
    - Scramble 2 eggs with 1/2 cup diced vegetables (e.g., spinach, tomatoes, and bell peppers). Serve with a slice of whole grain toast.

- **Lunch: Hummus Wrap with Fresh Vegetables and a Side Salad**
    - Spread hummus on a whole wheat wrap and fill with sliced cucumbers, bell peppers, and shredded carrots. Serve with a side salad of mixed greens.

- **Dinner: Lentil and Vegetable Curry with Brown Rice**
    - Cook 1 cup lentils with diced tomatoes, curry powder, and mixed vegetables (e.g., spinach, peas, and bell peppers). Serve with 1/2 cup cooked brown rice.

Day 5

- **Breakfast: Chia Seed Pudding with Berries**
    - Mix 3 tablespoons chia seeds with 1 cup unsweetened almond milk and a touch of vanilla extract. Let sit overnight. Top with fresh berries.
- **Lunch: Grilled Veggie Sandwich with a Side of Quinoa Salad**
    - Grill vegetables (e.g., zucchini, bell peppers, and onions) and layer on whole grain bread with a spread of hummus. Serve with a side of quinoa salad.
- **Dinner: Baked Chicken Breast with Roasted Sweet Potatoes and Green Beans**
    - Bake a chicken breast with rosemary and garlic at 375°F (190°C) for 25 minutes. Serve with roasted sweet potatoes and steamed green beans.

Day 6

- **Breakfast: Smoothie with Kale, Pineapple, and Flaxseeds**
    - Blend 1 cup kale, 1 cup pineapple chunks, 1 tablespoon flaxseeds, and 1/2 cup unsweetened almond milk.
- **Lunch: Spinach and Feta Stuffed Chicken Breast with Mixed Vegetables**
    - Stuff a chicken breast with spinach and feta cheese, then bake at 375°F (190°C) for 25 minutes. Serve with a side of steamed mixed vegetables.
- **Dinner: Vegetable Stew with Whole Grain Bread**

- Simmer vegetables (e.g., carrots, potatoes, celery, and onions) in vegetable broth with herbs. Serve with a slice of whole grain bread.

Day 7

- **Breakfast: Greek Yogurt with Honey and Fresh Fruit**
    - Top 1 cup Greek yogurt with a drizzle of honey and a mix of fresh fruit (e.g., berries and sliced kiwi).
- **Lunch: Quinoa Pilaf with Roasted Vegetables**
    - Cook 1/2 cup quinoa with vegetable broth and mix with roasted vegetables (e.g., squash, bell peppers, and onions).
- **Dinner: Herb-Crusted Baked Fish with Steamed Asparagus**
    - Bake a fish fillet with a crust of herbs (e.g., parsley, thyme) at 375°F (190°C) for 20 minutes. Serve with steamed asparagus.

Week 1: Detox and Reset is designed to provide a gentle start to your liver-friendly journey. Emphasis is placed on fresh, whole foods that support detoxification and overall health. Each meal is carefully crafted to balance nutrients and promote liver function, helping you establish healthy eating habits from the very beginning.

Week 2: Nutrient Boost

In Week 2, the focus is on enhancing your nutrient intake with foods rich in vitamins, minerals, and antioxidants that support liver health. This week's meals are designed to be vibrant, satisfying, and packed with ingredients that provide a boost to your overall well-being.

Day 8

- **Breakfast: Berry Smoothie Bowl with Almond Butter**
    - Blend 1 cup mixed berries, 1 banana, 1/2 cup unsweetened almond milk, and 1 tablespoon almond butter. Top with granola, chia seeds, and fresh berries.
- **Lunch: Chickpea and Avocado Salad**
    - Mix 1 cup chickpeas with 1/2 avocado, diced tomatoes, cucumbers, and red onion. Dress with lemon juice, olive oil, salt, and pepper.
- **Dinner: Turkey and Vegetable Skillet with Brown Rice**
    - Sauté 4 oz ground turkey with 2 cups mixed vegetables (e.g., bell peppers, spinach, and zucchini) in 1 tablespoon olive oil. Serve with 1/2 cup cooked brown rice.

Day 9

- **Breakfast: Apple Cinnamon Oatmeal**
    - Cook 1/2 cup oats with 1 cup water or unsweetened almond milk. Stir in 1 chopped apple, 1 tablespoon chia seeds, and a sprinkle of cinnamon.
- **Lunch: Greek Salad with Grilled Chicken**

- Combine 2 cups mixed greens with 1/2 cup sliced grilled chicken, cherry tomatoes, cucumbers, olives, and feta cheese. Dress with olive oil and lemon juice.
- **Dinner: Baked Tilapia with Quinoa and Steamed Green Beans**
    - Bake tilapia fillets with lemon and herbs at 375°F (190°C) for 15 minutes. Serve with 1/2 cup cooked quinoa and steamed green beans.

Day 10

- **Breakfast: Avocado Toast with a Poached Egg**
    - Top a slice of whole grain toast with 1/2 avocado and a poached egg. Season with salt, pepper, and a sprinkle of red pepper flakes.
- **Lunch: Black Bean and Corn Salad**
    - Mix 1 cup black beans with 1 cup corn, diced red bell pepper, cherry tomatoes, and cilantro. Dress with lime juice, olive oil, salt, and pepper.
- **Dinner: Spaghetti Squash with Tomato Basil Sauce**
    - Roast spaghetti squash and top with homemade tomato basil sauce made from tomatoes, garlic, basil, and olive oil. Serve with a side of steamed spinach.

Day 11

- **Breakfast: Smoothie with Spinach, Banana, and Mango**
    - Blend 1 cup spinach, 1 banana, 1/2 cup mango, and 1/2 cup unsweetened almond milk. Add a tablespoon of flaxseeds for extra nutrition.

- **Lunch: Roasted Vegetable Wrap with Hummus**
    - Spread hummus on a whole wheat wrap and fill with roasted vegetables (e.g., bell peppers, zucchini, and onions). Roll up and serve with a side salad.
- **Dinner: Chicken and Sweet Potato Bake**
    - Bake 4 oz chicken breast with cubed sweet potatoes and a mix of your favorite herbs at 375°F (190°C) for 30 minutes. Serve with a side of steamed broccoli.

Day 12

- **Breakfast: Overnight Oats with Chia Seeds and Blueberries**
    - Combine 1/2 cup oats with 1 cup unsweetened almond milk, 1 tablespoon chia seeds, and 1/2 cup blueberries. Let sit overnight in the fridge.
- **Lunch: Lentil Salad with Cucumber, Bell Peppers, and Feta**
    - Toss 1 cup cooked lentils with diced cucumber, bell peppers, and 1/4 cup crumbled feta cheese. Dress with olive oil, lemon juice, salt, and pepper.
- **Dinner: Stir-Fried Tofu with Mixed Vegetables and Brown Rice**
    - Stir-fry 4 oz tofu with a mix of vegetables (e.g., snap peas, carrots, and bell peppers) in 1 tablespoon sesame oil. Serve with 1/2 cup cooked brown rice.

Day 13

- **Breakfast: Berry and Yogurt Parfait**

- Layer 1 cup Greek yogurt with 1/2 cup mixed berries and a tablespoon of granola. Drizzle with a small amount of honey if desired.

- **Lunch: Quinoa and Roasted Pepper Salad**
    - Mix 1/2 cup cooked quinoa with 1/2 cup roasted red peppers, cherry tomatoes, cucumbers, and a handful of fresh basil. Dress with balsamic vinegar and olive oil.

- **Dinner: Grilled Portobello Mushrooms with Steamed Broccoli**
    - Grill 2 large Portobello mushrooms with a touch of balsamic glaze. Serve with 1 cup steamed broccoli and a side of quinoa.

Day 14

- **Breakfast: Green Smoothie with Kale, Apple, and Cucumber**
    - Blend 1 cup kale, 1 apple, 1/2 cucumber, and 1/2 cup unsweetened almond milk. Add a tablespoon of chia seeds for extra nutrients.

- **Lunch: Turkey and Avocado Lettuce Wraps**
    - Wrap 4 oz sliced turkey and 1/2 avocado in large lettuce leaves. Add sliced tomatoes and a touch of mustard or hummus if desired.

- **Dinner: Baked Cod with a Side of Quinoa and Sautéed Spinach** o   Bake cod fillets with a sprinkle of lemon and dill at 375°F (190°C) for 20 minutes. Serve with 1/2 cup cooked quinoa and sautéed spinach.

Week 2: Nutrient Boost focuses on increasing your intake of vital nutrients to support liver health. The meals are designed to be rich in vitamins, minerals, and antioxidants, featuring a variety of colorful fruits, vegetables, and lean proteins. Each day provides a balanced approach to eating that helps optimize liver function while keeping your diet diverse and enjoyable. Adjust portion sizes and ingredients to fit your personal preferences and nutritional needs.

Week 3: Balance and Sustain

In Week 3, the focus shifts to maintaining balance and sustainability in your liver-friendly diet. The meals are designed to be both nutritious and satisfying, helping you establish long-term eating habits that support liver health. This week's plan emphasizes balanced macronutrients, portion control, and diverse flavors.

Day 15

- **Breakfast: Chia Seed and Fruit Pudding**
    - o   Mix 3 tablespoons chia seeds with 1 cup unsweetened almond milk and a touch of vanilla extract. Let sit overnight. Top with fresh fruit such as kiwi and berries.
- **Lunch: Mediterranean Chickpea Salad**

- Toss 1 cup chickpeas with diced cucumbers, cherry tomatoes, red onion, olives, and feta cheese. Dress with olive oil, lemon juice, salt, and pepper.
- **Dinner: Stuffed Bell Peppers with Ground Turkey and Quinoa**
  - Stuff bell peppers with a mixture of 4 oz ground turkey, 1/2 cup cooked quinoa, diced tomatoes, and spices. Bake at 375°F (190°C) for 25 minutes.

Day 16

- **Breakfast: Green Smoothie with Kale, Pineapple, and Flaxseeds**
  - Blend 1 cup kale, 1 cup pineapple chunks, 1 tablespoon flaxseeds, and 1/2 cup unsweetened almond milk.
- **Lunch: Spinach and Strawberry Salad with Grilled Chicken**
  - Combine 2 cups spinach with 1/2 cup sliced grilled chicken, sliced strawberries, walnuts, and a light balsamic vinaigrette.
- **Dinner: Roasted Chicken Thighs with Quinoa and Steamed Carrots**
  - Roast chicken thighs with rosemary and garlic at 375°F (190°C) for 30 minutes. Serve with 1/2 cup cooked quinoa and steamed carrots.

Day 17

- **Breakfast: Banana and Walnut Oatmeal**
  - Cook 1/2 cup oats with 1 cup water or unsweetened almond milk. Stir in 1 sliced banana and 1/4 cup chopped walnuts. Sprinkle with cinnamon.

- **Lunch: Cucumber and Hummus Wrap**
    - Spread hummus on a whole wheat wrap and fill with sliced cucumbers, shredded carrots, and spinach. Roll up and serve with a side salad.
- **Dinner: Grilled Salmon with Roasted Sweet Potatoes and Green Beans**
    - Grill salmon fillets with lemon and herbs. Serve with 1/2 cup roasted sweet potatoes and steamed green beans.

Day 18

- **Breakfast: Smoothie Bowl with Avocado, Banana, and Mixed Berries**
    - Blend 1/2 avocado, 1 banana, 1/2 cup mixed berries, and 1/2 cup unsweetened almond milk. Top with granola and fresh fruit.
- **Lunch: Mediterranean Quinoa Salad**
    - Mix 1/2 cup cooked quinoa with diced tomatoes, cucumbers, olives, red onion, and feta cheese. Dress with olive oil, lemon juice, and oregano.
- **Dinner: Turkey Meatballs with Zucchini Noodles and Marinara Sauce**
    - Bake turkey meatballs at 375°F (190°C) for 20 minutes. Serve with zucchini noodles and marinara sauce made from tomatoes, garlic, and basil.

Day 19

- **Breakfast: Yogurt with Fresh Fruit and Granola**
    - Top 1 cup Greek yogurt with a mix of fresh fruit (e.g., berries, kiwi) and 2 tablespoons granola. Drizzle with a small amount of honey if desired.
- **Lunch: Roasted Vegetable and Quinoa Bowl**
    - Combine 1/2 cup cooked quinoa with roasted vegetables (e.g., bell peppers, squash, and onions). Top with a drizzle of balsamic glaze.
- **Dinner: Baked Chicken Breast with Steamed Broccoli and Brown Rice**
    - Bake chicken breast with herbs at 375°F (190°C) for 25 minutes. Serve with 1/2 cup steamed broccoli and 1/2 cup cooked brown rice.

Day 20

- **Breakfast: Overnight Chia Pudding with Raspberries**
    - Combine 3 tablespoons chia seeds with 1 cup unsweetened almond milk and a touch of vanilla. Let sit overnight. Top with fresh raspberries.
- **Lunch: Spinach and Feta Stuffed Bell Peppers**
    - Stuff bell peppers with a mixture of spinach, feta cheese, and cooked quinoa. Bake at 375°F (190°C) for 20 minutes.

- **Dinner: Grilled Shrimp Skewers with Quinoa and Roasted Bell Peppers**
    - Grill shrimp skewers with a touch of olive oil and lemon juice. Serve with 1/2 cup cooked quinoa and roasted bell peppers.

Day 21

- **Breakfast: Green Smoothie with Spinach, Apple, and Pear**
    - Blend 1 cup spinach, 1 apple, 1 pear, and 1/2 cup unsweetened almond milk. Add a tablespoon of chia seeds for extra nutrients.
- **Lunch: Lentil and Spinach Salad**
    - Toss 1 cup cooked lentils with fresh spinach, cherry tomatoes, cucumbers, and a light lemon vinaigrette.
- **Dinner: Baked Cod with a Side of Quinoa and Sautéed Zucchini**
    - Bake cod fillets with lemon and herbs at 375°F (190°C) for 20 minutes. Serve with 1/2 cup cooked quinoa and sautéed zucchini.

Summary

Week 3: Balance and Sustain focuses on maintaining a balanced diet with sustainable eating habits. The meals this week are designed to provide steady energy, support liver health, and promote overall well-being. By incorporating a variety of nutrient-dense ingredients and balanced meals, you'll reinforce the healthy habits established in the previous weeks and prepare for the final stretch of your 30-day journey. Adjust portion sizes and ingredients according to personal preferences and nutritional needs.

In the final week of your 30-day liver-friendly meal plan, the focus is on maintaining the healthy habits you've established and ensuring long-term health. This week features a variety of satisfying and nutritious meals that reinforce liver-supportive eating patterns and keep your diet enjoyable and sustainable.

Day 22

- **Breakfast: Berry Chia Pudding**
    - Mix 3 tablespoons chia seeds with 1 cup unsweetened almond milk and a dash of vanilla extract. Let sit overnight. Top with a mix of fresh berries and a sprinkle of flaxseeds.
- **Lunch: Grilled Chicken and Avocado Salad**
    - Toss 2 cups mixed greens with 1/2 cup sliced grilled chicken, 1/2 avocado, cherry tomatoes, and a light vinaigrette made with olive oil and lemon juice.
- **Dinner: Baked Halibut with Sweet Potato Wedges and Steamed Brussels Sprouts**
    - Bake halibut fillets with a touch of lemon and dill at 375°F (190°C) for 20 minutes. Serve with 1/2 cup baked sweet potato wedges and steamed Brussels sprouts.

Day 23

- **Breakfast: Oatmeal with Pumpkin and Pecans**
    - Cook 1/2 cup oats with 1 cup water or unsweetened almond milk. Stir in 1/4 cup canned pumpkin, 1 tablespoon pecans, and a sprinkle of cinnamon.

- **Lunch: Quinoa and Roasted Vegetable Bowl**
    - Combine 1/2 cup cooked quinoa with roasted vegetables (e.g., bell peppers, zucchini, and carrots). Top with a drizzle of tahini sauce.
- **Dinner: Turkey and Spinach Stuffed Mushrooms**
    - Stuff large mushroom caps with a mixture of ground turkey, spinach, and garlic. Bake at 375°F (190°C) for 20 minutes. Serve with a side of mixed greens.

Day 24

- **Breakfast: Green Smoothie with Kale, Apple, and Celery**
    - Blend 1 cup kale, 1 apple, 2 celery stalks, and 1/2 cup unsweetened almond milk. Add a tablespoon of chia seeds for extra fiber.
- **Lunch: Lentil Soup with a Side Salad**
    - Prepare lentil soup with onions, carrots, celery, and tomatoes. Serve with a side salad of mixed greens and a simple olive oil and vinegar dressing.
- **Dinner: Baked Chicken with Roasted Asparagus and Quinoa**
    - Bake chicken breast with herbs at 375°F (190°C) for 25 minutes. Serve with 1/2 cup roasted asparagus and 1/2 cup cooked quinoa.

Day 25

- **Breakfast: Greek Yogurt with Fresh Fruit and Nuts**

- o Top 1 cup Greek yogurt with a mix of fresh fruit (e.g., berries, kiwi) and 2 tablespoons of chopped nuts (e.g., almonds or walnuts).

- **Lunch: Spinach and Feta Stuffed Chicken Breast**
  - o Stuff chicken breasts with a mixture of spinach and feta cheese. Bake at 375°F (190°C) for 30 minutes. Serve with a side of steamed green beans.

- **Dinner: Salmon Patties with Sweet Potato Mash**
  - o Mix canned salmon with eggs, oats, and herbs to form patties. Pan-fry or bake at 375°F (190°C) for 15 minutes. Serve with mashed sweet potatoes and a side of sautéed spinach.

Day 26

- **Breakfast: Smoothie Bowl with Mango, Banana, and Almonds**
  - o Blend 1/2 cup mango, 1 banana, and 1/2 cup unsweetened almond milk. Top with sliced almonds, chia seeds, and a few fresh berries.

- **Lunch: Cucumber and Avocado Wrap**
  - o Spread hummus on a whole wheat wrap and layer with sliced cucumber, avocado, and shredded carrots. Roll up and serve with a side of cherry tomatoes.

- **Dinner: Grilled Portobello Mushrooms with Quinoa and Steamed Broccoli**
  - o Grill Portobello mushrooms with balsamic vinegar. Serve with 1/2 cup cooked quinoa and steamed broccoli.

Day 27

- **Breakfast: Apple Cinnamon Overnight Oats**
    - Combine 1/2 cup oats with 1 cup unsweetened almond milk, 1 chopped apple, and a sprinkle of cinnamon. Let sit overnight in the fridge.
- **Lunch: Roasted Beet and Goat Cheese Salad**
    - Toss roasted beets with mixed greens, goat cheese, walnuts, and a balsamic vinaigrette.
- **Dinner: Turkey and Vegetable Stir-Fry**
    - Stir-fry 4 oz ground turkey with a mix of vegetables (e.g., bell peppers, broccoli, and snow peas) in 1 tablespoon olive oil. Serve with 1/2 cup cooked brown rice.

Day 28

- **Breakfast: Chia Seed and Berry Parfait**
    - Layer 1/2 cup Greek yogurt with chia seed pudding (3 tablespoons chia seeds mixed with 1 cup almond milk), and top with fresh berries.
- **Lunch: Quinoa Salad with Avocado and Black Beans**
    - Mix 1/2 cup cooked quinoa with 1/2 cup black beans, 1/2 avocado, diced tomatoes, and cilantro. Dress with lime juice and olive oil.
- **Dinner: Baked Cod with a Side of Roasted Vegetables and Brown Rice**
    - Bake cod fillets with lemon and herbs at 375°F (190°C) for 20 minutes. Serve with 1/2 cup roasted vegetables (e.g., carrots, bell peppers) and 1/2 cup cooked brown rice.

Day 29

- **Breakfast: Berry and Spinach Smoothie**
    - Blend 1 cup spinach, 1/2 cup mixed berries, 1 banana, and 1/2 cup unsweetened almond milk. Add a tablespoon of flaxseeds for added nutrients.

- **Lunch: Grilled Veggie and Hummus Wrap**
    - Spread hummus on a whole wheat wrap and fill with grilled vegetables (e.g., zucchini, bell peppers, and onions). Roll up and serve with a side of mixed greens.

- **Dinner: Stuffed Acorn Squash with Lentils and Spinach**
    - Roast acorn squash halves and stuff with a mixture of cooked lentils, spinach, and spices. Bake at 375°F (190°C) for 20 minutes.

Day 30

- **Breakfast: Pumpkin Spice Smoothie**
    - Blend 1/2 cup canned pumpkin with 1 banana, 1/2 cup unsweetened almond milk, and a sprinkle of pumpkin spice. Add a tablespoon of chia seeds if desired.

- **Lunch: Chicken and Avocado Salad with Citrus Vinaigrette**
    - Toss 2 cups mixed greens with 1/2 cup grilled chicken, 1/2 avocado, orange slices, and a citrus vinaigrette made with olive oil, lemon juice, and orange zest.

- **Dinner: Grilled Shrimp with Quinoa and Steamed Asparagus**

- Grill shrimp skewers with a touch of garlic and lime. Serve with 1/2 cup cooked quinoa and steamed asparagus.

Week 4: Maintenance and Long-Term Health aims to solidify the healthy habits you've developed over the past month. The meals this week continue to support liver health while offering variety and balance. By focusing on diverse, nutrient-dense ingredients and maintaining enjoyable eating patterns, you can sustain the benefits of a liver-friendly diet and support your overall well-being long-term. Adjust portion sizes and ingredients according to your preferences and nutritional needs.

Chapter 10: Lifestyle Methods for a Healthy Liver

Exercise and Physical Activity

Regular exercise and physical activity are fundamental components of a healthy lifestyle, and they play a significant role in maintaining liver health. Engaging in appropriate types of exercise can help manage weight, reduce liver fat, enhance liver function, and prevent the onset of liver diseases. Below is an extensive guide on how exercise and physical activity contribute to liver health, including specific types of exercises that are beneficial and tips on creating an effective exercise routine.

Types of Exercises Beneficial for Liver Health

1. Aerobic Exercise

Aerobic exercise, also known as cardiovascular exercise, is any activity that increases your heart rate and improves circulation. This type of exercise is highly effective in reducing liver fat and improving liver function.

- **Examples:**
    - **Walking:** A brisk 30-minute walk daily can help improve overall cardiovascular health and aid in liver fat reduction.
    - **Jogging or Running:** More intense than walking, jogging or running can significantly impact liver health by promoting fat metabolism.
    - **Cycling:** Whether stationary or on the road, cycling is an excellent way to get cardiovascular exercise and boost overall fitness.
    - **Swimming:** This low-impact exercise provides a full-body workout that enhances cardiovascular health and burns calories efficiently.

Benefits:

- Reduces liver fat, particularly in cases of non-alcoholic fatty liver disease (NAFLD).
- Improves insulin sensitivity, which helps prevent liver-related conditions.

- Enhances overall cardiovascular health, reducing the risk of hypertension and heart disease.

2. Strength Training

Strength training, also known as resistance training, involves exercises that build muscle mass and strength. Building muscle helps improve metabolic rate and supports healthy liver function.

- **Examples:**
    - **Weightlifting:** Using free weights or machines to target major muscle groups can help improve muscle tone and metabolic health.
    - **Bodyweight Exercises:** Push-ups, squats, lunges, and planks are effective for building strength without needing equipment.
    - **Resistance Bands:** These provide a versatile way to perform strength training exercises at home or while traveling.

Benefits:

- Increases muscle mass, which boosts metabolism and aids in fat burning.
- Helps regulate blood sugar levels, reducing the risk of type 2 diabetes and associated liver issues.
- Supports overall body composition by reducing visceral fat around the liver.

3. Flexibility and Stretching

Flexibility exercises improve range of motion and reduce muscle stiffness. While not directly impacting liver function, they are crucial for overall physical health and well-being.

- **Examples:**
    - **Yoga:** Incorporates stretching, breathing, and balance exercises that improve flexibility, reduce stress, and support overall health.
    - **Pilates:** Focuses on core strength and flexibility, enhancing overall body stability and alignment.

Benefits:

- Reduces muscle tension and improves mobility.
- Helps prevent injuries related to other forms of exercise.
- Promotes relaxation and reduces stress, which can indirectly benefit liver health.

4. High-Intensity Interval Training (HIIT)

HIIT involves short bursts of intense exercise followed by rest periods. This type of training is highly effective for improving cardiovascular fitness and burning calories.

- **Examples:**
    - **Interval Running:** Alternating between sprinting and walking or jogging.
    - **Circuit Training:** Performing a series of exercises targeting different muscle groups with minimal rest between them.

Benefits:

- Burns a significant number of calories in a short period, aiding in weight management.
- Improves cardiovascular health and insulin sensitivity.
- Can be adapted to various fitness levels and preferences.

Creating an Exercise Routine

1. Assess Your Current Fitness Level

Before starting a new exercise routine, evaluate your current fitness level and any potential health concerns. This assessment will help you determine appropriate exercises and intensity levels.

- **Self-Assessment:** Consider how often you currently exercise, your physical capabilities, and any existing health conditions.
- **Consult a Professional:** If you have chronic health issues or are new to exercise, consult a healthcare provider or fitness professional for personalized recommendations.

2. Set Realistic Goals

Establish clear, achievable goals to keep you motivated and track your progress. Goals should be specific, measurable, attainable, relevant, and time-bound (SMART).

- **Examples:**
    - Aim to exercise for 30 minutes a day, five days a week.
    - Set a goal to improve your strength by lifting heavier weights over a period of months.

3. Plan Your Routine

Design a well-rounded exercise routine that incorporates various types of exercise, including aerobic, strength, and flexibility training. Balance different types of activities to ensure comprehensive fitness benefits.

- **Sample Weekly Plan:**
    - **Monday:** 30 minutes of brisk walking or jogging.
    - **Tuesday:** Strength training focusing on upper body muscles.
    - **Wednesday:** Yoga or stretching session for flexibility.
    - **Thursday:** 30 minutes of cycling or swimming.
    - **Friday:** Strength training focusing on lower body muscles.
    - **Saturday:** High-intensity interval training (HIIT) or a recreational sport.
    - **Sunday:** Rest day or gentle stretching.
-

4. Incorporate Variety and Fun

To maintain interest and motivation, include a variety of exercises and activities that you enjoy. Engaging in activities that are enjoyable increases the likelihood of sticking with your routine.

- **Ideas:**
    - Join a fitness class or sports team.
    - Try new forms of exercise, such as dance or martial arts.
    - Exercise with friends or family for added social support and enjoyment.

5. Monitor Your Progress

Keep track of your exercise routine and progress to stay motivated and make necessary adjustments. Use a journal, fitness app, or wearable device to monitor key metrics such as workout duration, intensity, and improvements in strength or endurance.

- **Tracking Methods:**
    - Record workout details in a journal or app.
    - Use a fitness tracker to monitor steps, heart rate, and calories burned.
    - Periodically assess your progress toward your fitness goals.

6. Listen to Your Body

Pay attention to how your body responds to exercise and adjust your routine as needed. Rest and recovery are essential to prevent overtraining and injuries.

- **Signs of Overtraining:** Fatigue, persistent soreness, irritability, and decreased performance.
- **Recovery Tips:** Incorporate rest days, ensure adequate sleep, and stay hydrated.

Summary

Exercise and physical activity are crucial for maintaining liver health and overall well-being. Engaging in a variety of exercises, including aerobic, strength, flexibility, and high-intensity interval training, can help reduce liver fat, improve metabolic health, and support overall fitness. Creating a balanced exercise routine, setting realistic goals, incorporating variety, and monitoring progress are essential for achieving long-term success. By integrating regular physical activity into your lifestyle, you can support liver health and enhance your quality of life.

Stress Management

Managing stress is a crucial aspect of maintaining liver health and overall well-being. Chronic stress can have a significant impact on the liver, leading to inflammation, fat accumulation, and an increased risk of liver diseases. Effective stress management techniques, along with ensuring adequate sleep and relaxation, play a vital role in supporting liver function and improving quality of life. Below is an in-depth look at techniques for reducing stress and the importance of sleep and relaxation.

Techniques for Reducing Stress

1. Mindfulness and Meditation

Mindfulness and **meditation** are practices that help focus the mind and promote relaxation. These techniques can lower stress levels, reduce anxiety, and improve overall mental health, which indirectly benefits liver health.

- **Mindfulness:** Involves paying attention to the present moment without judgment. Practicing mindfulness can help reduce stress and promote emotional balance.
- **Meditation:** Includes various forms such as guided meditation, transcendental meditation, and mindfulness meditation. Regular meditation practice has been shown to reduce stress and improve mental clarity.

How to Practice:

- Start with short sessions of 5-10 minutes daily.

- Use meditation apps or guided recordings if needed.
- Create a quiet space for practice and focus on your breathing or a specific mantra.

2. Deep Breathing Exercises

Deep breathing exercises help activate the body's relaxation response and can significantly reduce stress levels. These exercises help calm the nervous system and promote a sense of tranquility.

- **Techniques:**
    - **Diaphragmatic Breathing:** Breathe deeply into your abdomen rather than shallow breaths into your chest. Inhale for 4 seconds, hold for 4 seconds, and exhale for 4 seconds.
    - **Box Breathing:** Inhale for 4 seconds, hold for 4 seconds, exhale for 4 seconds, and hold for another 4 seconds. Repeat as needed.

How to Practice:

- Find a comfortable seated position.
- Focus on slow, deep breaths, and try to clear your mind of distractions.
- Practice for 5-10 minutes, several times a day if possible.

3. Physical Activity

Regular exercise is a powerful stress reliever. Physical activity releases endorphins, which are natural mood lifters, and helps alleviate feelings of stress and anxiety.

- **Examples:**

- **Aerobic Exercises:** Activities like walking, running, or cycling.
- **Strength Training:** Weightlifting or bodyweight exercises.
- **Relaxing Activities:** Yoga and stretching can also help reduce stress.

How to Incorporate:

- Aim for at least 30 minutes of moderate exercise most days of the week.
- Choose activities that you enjoy to make exercise a regular part of your routine.

4. Social Support and Connection

Maintaining strong social connections can help buffer the effects of stress. Spending time with friends and family, and engaging in social activities can provide emotional support and improve mood.

- **Ways to Connect:**
  - **Social Activities:** Join clubs, participate in community events, or attend social gatherings.
  - **Support Networks:** Seek out support groups or therapy if needed.
  - **Communication:** Regularly check in with loved ones and share your feelings.

5. Hobbies and Leisure Activities

Engaging in hobbies and activities you enjoy can provide a mental break from stressors and enhance overall well-being.

- **Examples:**

- **Creative Outlets:** Painting, writing, or playing music.
- **Relaxing Activities:** Reading, gardening, or cooking.
- **Physical Hobbies:** Dancing or hiking.

How to Integrate:

- Set aside time each week for activities that you find fulfilling.
- Balance these activities with other responsibilities to ensure they are a regular part of your life.

6. Healthy Eating Habits

A balanced diet can help manage stress by providing essential nutrients that support brain function and overall health.

- **Nutrient-Rich Foods:**
    - **Omega-3 Fatty Acids:** Found in fish, flaxseeds, and walnuts.
    - **Antioxidants:** Found in fruits and vegetables.
    - **Complex Carbohydrates:** Found in whole grains, legumes, and vegetables.

How to Apply:

- Include a variety of nutrient-dense foods in your diet.
- Avoid excessive caffeine and sugar, which can exacerbate stress.

7. Time Management

Effective time management can help reduce stress by organizing tasks and reducing feelings of overwhelm.

- **Strategies:**

- **Prioritization:** Make a list of tasks and prioritize them based on importance and deadlines.
- **Scheduling:** Use a planner or digital calendar to manage appointments and deadlines.
- **Break Tasks:** Break larger tasks into smaller, manageable steps.

How to Implement:

- Plan your day or week in advance.
- Allocate specific times for work, relaxation, and personal activities.

Importance of Sleep and Relaxation

1. Role of Sleep in Liver Health

Adequate sleep is essential for overall health, including liver function. Poor sleep can lead to metabolic disturbances, increased liver fat accumulation, and a higher risk of liver diseases.

- **Effects of Sleep Deprivation:**
  - **Metabolic Disruption:** Can lead to insulin resistance and increased liver fat.
  - **Increased Stress Hormones:** Higher levels of cortisol can negatively impact liver health.
  - **Impaired Liver Repair:** The liver performs critical repair and detoxification functions during sleep.

Tips for Quality Sleep:

- **Establish a Routine:** Go to bed and wake up at the same time every day.

- **Create a Relaxing Environment:** Keep your bedroom cool, dark, and quiet.
- **Limit Screen Time:** Avoid screens at least an hour before bed to reduce blue light exposure.

2. Importance of Relaxation

Relaxation techniques help reduce stress and promote a state of calm, which supports liver health. Chronic stress can lead to increased inflammation and liver damage, making relaxation an important component of liver care.

- **Benefits of Relaxation:**
    - **Reduces Stress Hormones:** Helps lower levels of cortisol and adrenaline.
    - **Promotes Emotional Well-Being:** Enhances mood and reduces feelings of anxiety.
    - **Supports Liver Function:** Aids in detoxification and reduces the risk of stress-related liver conditions.

Relaxation Techniques:

- **Progressive Muscle Relaxation:** Involves tensing and then relaxing different muscle groups to reduce physical tension.
- **Guided Imagery:** Uses visualization techniques to create a mental escape from stress.
- **Aromatherapy:** Uses essential oils such as lavender or chamomile to promote relaxation.

How to Integrate Relaxation:

- Incorporate relaxation techniques into your daily routine, especially during stressful times.
- Use relaxation practices before bedtime to improve sleep quality.

Stress management is essential for maintaining liver health and overall well-being. Techniques such as mindfulness, deep breathing, physical activity, social support, hobbies, healthy eating, and effective time management can help reduce stress levels. Additionally, prioritizing quality sleep and incorporating relaxation techniques are crucial for supporting liver function and overall health. By integrating these stress management strategies into your lifestyle, you can enhance your liver health, improve your quality of life, and promote long-term wellness.

Avoiding Toxins

The liver plays a crucial role in detoxifying the body, processing chemicals, and filtering out harmful substances. Reducing exposure to toxins and choosing liver-friendly products can significantly support liver health and reduce the burden on this vital organ. Below is an in-depth guide on avoiding toxins through reducing exposure to environmental toxins and selecting liver-friendly household products.

Reducing Exposure to Environmental Toxins

1. Air Quality Management

Indoor and outdoor air pollution can negatively impact liver health. Poor air quality can contribute to inflammation and oxidative stress, which may burden the liver.

- **Indoor Air Quality:**
    - **Ventilation:** Ensure proper ventilation by opening windows and using exhaust fans to reduce indoor air pollutants.
    - **Air Purifiers:** Use air purifiers with HEPA filters to remove airborne particles, allergens, and toxins.
    - **Houseplants:** Certain houseplants, such as spider plants and peace lilies, can help improve indoor air quality by absorbing toxins.
- **Outdoor Air Quality:**
    - **Avoid High Pollution Areas:** Limit outdoor activities during high pollution periods or in heavily industrialized areas.
    - **Use Masks:** Consider using air pollution masks in areas with high levels of smog or particulate matter.

2. Water Quality

Contaminated water can expose the liver to harmful chemicals and pathogens. Ensuring clean and safe drinking water is essential for liver health.

- **Filtration:** Use water filters that remove contaminants such as chlorine, heavy metals, and pesticides. Consider reverse osmosis systems for comprehensive filtration.
- **Regular Testing:** Have your water tested for contaminants if you rely on well water or live in areas with known water quality issues.

- **Avoid Plastic Bottles:** Reduce the use of single-use plastic bottles, which can leach harmful chemicals into the water.

3. Chemical Exposure

Reducing exposure to harmful chemicals found in various products can help lower the toxic load on the liver.

- **Pesticides and Herbicides:** Opt for organic produce when possible to avoid pesticide residues. Wash fruits and vegetables thoroughly to remove contaminants.
- **Heavy Metals:** Minimize consumption of fish known to have high levels of mercury, such as shark or swordfish. Choose seafood that is lower in mercury.

4. Reducing Exposure to Industrial Chemicals

Industrial chemicals, such as solvents and heavy metals, can be found in everyday items and environments.

- **Protective Gear:** Use appropriate protective gear when working with chemicals or in environments with high exposure risks.
- **Label Awareness:** Be aware of and avoid products with labels indicating high levels of volatile organic compounds (VOCs) or other harmful chemicals.

Choosing Liver-Friendly Household Products

1. Cleaning Products

Many conventional cleaning products contain harsh chemicals that can contribute to liver stress and overall health issues. Opt for liver-friendly and non-toxic alternatives.

- **Natural Cleaners:** Choose cleaning products made from natural ingredients, such as vinegar, baking soda, and lemon juice. These are effective and safer alternatives to chemical-based cleaners.
- **Eco-Friendly Brands:** Look for cleaning products labeled as eco-friendly or biodegradable. These products are generally less harmful to both health and the environment.

2. Personal Care Products

Personal care products, such as shampoos, lotions, and cosmetics, often contain chemicals that can be absorbed through the skin and impact liver health.

- **Chemical-Free Products:** Opt for personal care products free of parabens, sulfates, phthalates, and synthetic fragrances. Look for products labeled as natural or organic.
- **DIY Options:** Consider making your own personal care products using natural ingredients. For example, you can create facial scrubs or body lotions with ingredients like coconut oil and essential oils.

3. Home Furnishings

Certain home furnishings, such as carpets, furniture, and paints, can emit volatile organic compounds (VOCs) that may affect liver health.

- **Low-VOC Paints:** Choose paints and finishes labeled as low-VOC or no-VOC to minimize exposure to harmful chemicals during home renovation.

- **Natural Materials:** Opt for furniture and flooring made from natural materials, such as wood, bamboo, or organic cotton, which are less likely to contain toxic chemicals.

4. Food Storage

How food is stored and prepared can also impact liver health. Avoiding exposure to harmful chemicals from food storage containers is important.

- **Glass or Stainless Steel Containers:** Use glass or stainless steel containers for food storage instead of plastic. These materials do not leach chemicals into food.
- **Avoid Non-Stick Cookware:** Minimize use of non-stick cookware that contains polytetrafluoroethylene (PTFE) or perfluorooctanoic acid (PFOA), which can release harmful fumes when heated.

5. Pest Control

Traditional pest control methods often involve chemicals that can be harmful to both health and the environment.

- **Natural Pest Control:** Use natural pest control methods, such as essential oils, diatomaceous earth, or biological pest control (e.g., introducing beneficial insects).
- **Integrated Pest Management (IPM):** Consider IPM techniques, which combine preventive measures with minimal chemical use to manage pests effectively.

6. Air Fresheners

Commercial air fresheners often contain synthetic fragrances and chemicals that can impact liver health and overall well-being.

- **Natural Alternatives:** Use natural air fresheners such as essential oils (e.g., lavender or eucalyptus) or simmer pots with herbs and spices to freshen the air.
- **Ventilation:** Improve air quality through proper ventilation rather than relying on air fresheners.

Avoiding toxins is a vital aspect of maintaining liver health and overall well-being. Reducing exposure to environmental toxins, such as air and water pollutants, and choosing liver-friendly household products can significantly support liver function and reduce the toxic burden on the body. By adopting practices such as improving air and water quality, using natural and non-toxic products, and opting for safer food storage and pest control methods, you can create a healthier living environment that supports liver health. Integrating these lifestyle methods into your daily routine can enhance your overall well-being and promote long-term liver health.

Regular Medical Check-Ups

Maintaining liver health is not solely about lifestyle choices and diet; regular medical check-ups play a crucial role in early detection, prevention, and management of liver conditions. Regular screenings and understanding test results can help monitor liver function, catch potential issues early, and ensure timely intervention. Here's a comprehensive guide on the importance of regular screenings and understanding your test results.

Importance of Regular Screenings

1. Early Detection of Liver Diseases

Many liver diseases develop gradually and may not present noticeable symptoms until they are advanced. Regular screenings can detect liver problems early, allowing for prompt treatment and better outcomes.

- **Asymptomatic Conditions:** Conditions like non-alcoholic fatty liver disease (NAFLD) and hepatitis can progress silently. Early detection through screenings can prevent progression to more serious stages like cirrhosis or liver cancer.
- **Routine Check-Ups:** Regular liver function tests (LFTs) can identify abnormal liver enzyme levels, which may indicate underlying liver issues even if no symptoms are present.

2. Monitoring Chronic Liver Conditions

For individuals with chronic liver conditions such as hepatitis or cirrhosis, regular medical check-ups are essential for monitoring disease progression and adjusting treatment plans as needed.

- **Disease Management:** Regular monitoring helps assess the effectiveness of treatments, manage symptoms, and adjust medications or therapies.
- **Preventing Complications:** Monitoring can help prevent complications associated with chronic liver diseases, such as liver failure or portal hypertension.

3. Assessing Risk Factors

Screenings can help assess risk factors for liver diseases, including those related to lifestyle, genetics, and underlying health conditions.

- **Risk Assessment:** Evaluate factors such as obesity, alcohol consumption, and family history to determine the need for more frequent or specific tests.

- **Preventive Measures:** Identifying risk factors early can lead to lifestyle changes or preventive measures to mitigate the risk of developing liver diseases.

4. Establishing Baseline Health

Regular check-ups establish a baseline for liver health, which is useful for comparing future test results and detecting any deviations from normal.

- **Baseline Data:** Initial tests provide reference points for evaluating changes in liver function over time.
- **Long-Term Monitoring:** Regular follow-ups help track trends and changes in liver health, providing valuable information for managing and preventing liver conditions.

Understanding Your Test Results

1. Liver Function Tests (LFTs)

Liver function tests are blood tests used to assess how well the liver is working and to detect liver inflammation or damage.

- **Common LFTs:**
    - **Alanine Aminotransferase (ALT):** Elevated levels may indicate liver inflammation or damage.
    - **Aspartate Aminotransferase (AST):** Increased levels can signal liver or muscle damage.
    - **Alkaline Phosphatase (ALP):** High levels may suggest bile duct obstruction or liver disease.
    - **Gamma-Glutamyl Transferase (GGT):** Elevated levels can indicate liver disease, bile duct issues, or alcohol use.

Interpreting Results:

- **Normal Ranges:** Each test has a reference range. Results outside this range may indicate liver problems but require further evaluation.
- **Context Matters:** Elevated levels may not always indicate a specific liver disease and can be influenced by other factors such as medications, infections, or exercise.

2. Imaging Tests

Imaging tests help visualize the liver's structure and identify abnormalities.

- **Ultrasound:** Commonly used to assess liver size, detect fatty liver, cysts, or tumors.
- **CT Scan (Computed Tomography):** Provides detailed cross-sectional images to detect tumors or liver damage.
- **MRI (Magnetic Resonance Imaging):** Offers detailed images of liver tissue and can assess liver fibrosis or cirrhosis.

Interpreting Results:

- **Normal Findings:** Indicate no visible abnormalities.
- **Abnormal Findings:** May require further diagnostic procedures, such as biopsy, or intervention based on the nature of the abnormalities.

3. Liver Biopsy

A liver biopsy involves taking a small sample of liver tissue for examination. It is used to diagnose liver diseases, assess the extent of damage, and guide treatment decisions.

- **Types of Biopsy:**

- **Percutaneous Biopsy:** A needle is inserted through the skin to collect a liver sample.
- **Transjugular Biopsy:** A catheter is inserted through a vein in the neck to obtain a liver sample.

Interpreting Results:

- **Histological Analysis:** Helps determine the presence and extent of liver diseases such as hepatitis, fibrosis, or cirrhosis.
- **Treatment Decisions:** Results guide treatment plans and management strategies based on the severity of liver damage.

4. Viral Hepatitis Tests

For those at risk of hepatitis, specific tests can determine the presence of hepatitis viruses (A, B, C) and assess liver function.

- **Hepatitis A, B, C Tests:** Detect antibodies or viral RNA to diagnose infections.
- **Hepatitis B Surface Antigen (HBsAg):** Indicates active hepatitis B infection.
- **HCV RNA Test:** Measures the amount of hepatitis C virus in the blood.

Interpreting Results:

- **Positive Results:** Indicate current or past infections and may require further testing or treatment.
- **Negative Results:** Typically mean no active infection, but confirmatory testing may be needed for comprehensive assessment.

5. Understanding Trends and Changes

Regular check-ups provide trends and changes in liver health over time. Understanding these trends helps manage and prevent liver diseases more effectively.

- **Trend Analysis:** Compare current results with previous ones to identify worsening or improving conditions.
- **Proactive Management:** Use trends to adjust lifestyle changes, treatment plans, or preventive measures.

Regular medical check-ups are essential for maintaining liver health and managing potential liver conditions. Through early detection, monitoring chronic diseases, assessing risk factors, and establishing baseline health, regular screenings can significantly improve outcomes and prevent complications. Understanding test results, including liver function tests, imaging tests, liver biopsy, and viral hepatitis tests, is crucial for effective management and treatment. By incorporating regular medical evaluations into your routine, you support your liver health and overall well-being, ensuring timely intervention and optimal health outcomes.

Chapter 11: Conclusion: Embracing a Healthy Liver Lifestyle

As we conclude our journey through the realm of liver health, it's essential to reflect on the key principles and practices that can profoundly impact our well-being. This cookbook has provided a comprehensive guide to nurturing your liver through diet, lifestyle changes, and mindful practices. By integrating these strategies into your daily life, you are not only enhancing your liver function but also promoting overall health and vitality.

The Importance of a Holistic Approach

Maintaining liver health requires a holistic approach that encompasses various aspects of life. It is not merely about following a specific diet or routine but about creating a balanced, sustainable lifestyle that supports the liver's critical functions. The liver is a remarkable organ with a significant role in metabolism, detoxification, and nutrient storage. Thus, caring for it involves addressing multiple facets of health, including nutrition, physical activity, stress management, and toxin avoidance.

Key Takeaways for a Liver-Friendly Lifestyle

1. Embrace a Balanced Diet

A liver-friendly diet focuses on whole, nutrient-dense foods that support liver function and overall health. Incorporating a variety of vegetables, fruits, whole grains, lean proteins, and healthy fats provides the essential nutrients the liver needs to function optimally. The recipes provided in this cookbook—from smoothie bowls and oatmeal variations to hearty soups and healthy desserts—are designed to offer delicious and nutritious options that align with liver health principles.

2. Prioritize Physical Activity

Regular exercise is vital for maintaining a healthy liver. It helps regulate body weight, reduce liver fat, and improve metabolic function. Incorporate both aerobic exercises and strength training into your routine, and find activities that you enjoy. Whether it's a daily walk, a yoga session, or a dance class, physical activity plays a crucial role in supporting liver health and overall well-being.

3. Manage Stress Effectively

Chronic stress can negatively impact liver health, leading to inflammation and other issues. Employ stress management techniques such as mindfulness, deep breathing, and relaxation exercises to reduce stress levels. Ensure you also get adequate sleep, as it is essential for liver repair and overall health. Prioritizing relaxation and stress reduction will help maintain balance and support liver function.

4. Avoid Toxins

Reducing exposure to environmental toxins and choosing liver-friendly household products can significantly support liver health. Be mindful of air and water quality, opt for natural cleaning and personal care products, and avoid harmful chemicals. By creating a healthier living environment, you reduce the toxic burden on your liver and promote overall well-being.

5. Commit to Regular Check-Ups

Regular medical check-ups are vital for early detection and management of liver conditions. Routine screenings, understanding test results, and monitoring liver health through medical evaluations ensure that potential issues are addressed promptly. Establish a proactive approach to health by scheduling regular check-ups and working closely with your healthcare provider.

Implementing Lifestyle Changes

Making lasting lifestyle changes involves setting realistic goals and gradually incorporating new habits into your daily routine. Start by focusing on one area, such as improving your diet, and build on your successes over time. Remember that consistency is key, and small, sustainable changes can lead to significant improvements in liver health and overall well-being.

1. Set Achievable Goals

Begin with achievable goals that fit your lifestyle and preferences. Whether it's incorporating more fruits and vegetables into your diet, increasing physical activity, or reducing stress, setting clear and manageable objectives will help you stay motivated and on track.

2. Monitor Your Progress

Keep track of your progress and celebrate your achievements along the way. Regularly reviewing your goals and reflecting on your accomplishments can help you stay focused and motivated. Adjust your approach as needed based on your experiences and feedback.

3. Seek Support

Engage with support networks, whether through friends, family, or online communities, to share experiences and gain encouragement. Having a support system can provide motivation, accountability, and practical advice for maintaining a healthy lifestyle.

Looking Forward

As you embark on your journey toward optimal liver health, remember that this is a lifelong commitment. Embracing a liver-friendly diet and lifestyle is not a temporary fix but a fundamental aspect of long-term well-being. By integrating the principles outlined in this cookbook into your daily life, you are making a positive investment in your health and future.

The path to a healthier liver is paved with mindful choices, balanced habits, and a proactive approach to well-being. Embrace this journey with enthusiasm and dedication, knowing that every step you take contributes to a healthier, more vibrant you.

Thank You

Thank you for allowing this cookbook to be a part of your journey toward better liver health. May the knowledge and recipes within these pages inspire you to make positive changes and embrace a lifestyle that supports and nourishes your liver. Here's to your health and well-being—cheers to a vibrant, liver-friendly life!

Printed in Great Britain
by Amazon